THE NEW AMERICAN WRITING:
Essays on American Literature
Since 1970

THE NEW AMERICAN WRITING:
Essays on American Literature Since 1970

edited by

Graham Clarke

VISION PRESS · LONDON
ST. MARTIN'S PRESS · NEW YORK

Vision Press Ltd.
c/o Vine House Distribution
Waldenbury, North Common
Chailey, E. Sussex BN8 4DR

and

St. Martin's Press, Inc.
175 Fifth Avenue
New York
N.Y. 10010

ISBN (UK) 0 85478 396 2
ISBN (US) 0 312 03566 7

British Library Cataloguing-in-Publication Data
The New American writing: essays on American literature
  since 1970.
  1. English literature. American writers, 1970–.
  Critical studies
  I. Clarke, Graham, 1948–
  810'.9'0054
  ISBN 0-85478-396-2

Library of Congress Cataloging-in-Publication Data
New American writing.
  (Critical studies series)
  1. American literature—20th century—History and
  criticism. I. Clarke, Graham. II. Series.
  PS225.N48 1990   810.9'0054   80-70056
  ISBN 0-312-03566-7 (St. Martin's)

Printed and bound in Great Britain by
Billing & Sons, Worcester.
Typeset by Galleon Photosetting,
Ipswich, Suffolk.
MCMLXXXX

Contents

Introduction

by GRAHAM CLARKE

The contemporary American writer is in no way a part of the social and political scene. He is therefore not muzzled, for no one fears his bite; nor is he called upon to compose. Whatever work he does must proceed from a reckless inner need. The world does not beckon, nor does it greatly reward. This is not a boast or a complaint. It is a fact. Serious writing must nowadays be written for the sake of the art. The condition I describe is not extraordinary. Certain scientists, philosophers, historians, and many mathematicians do the same, advancing their causes as they can. One must be satisfied with that.

> —William Gass, Preface to *In the Heart of the Heart of the Country and Other Stories* (1976)

The daily newspapers, then, fill us with wonder and awe (is it possible? is it happening?), also with sickness and despair. The fixes, the scandals, the insanity, the idiocy, the piety, the lies, the noise. . . . Recently, in *Commentary* Bejamin DeMott wrote that the 'deeply lodged suspicion of the times [is] namely, that events and individuals are unreal, and that power to alter the course of the age, of my life and your life, is actually vested nowhere.' There seems to be, said DeMott, a kind of 'universal descent into unreality'. The other night—to give a benign example of the descent—my wife turned on the radio and heard the announcer offering a series of cash prizes for the three best television plays of five minutes' duration written by children. It is difficult at such moments to find one's way around the kitchen. Certainly few days go by when incidents far less benign fail to remind us of what DeMott is talking about. When Edmund Wilson says that after reading *Life* magazine he feels he does not belong to the country depicted there, that he does not live in this country, I understand what he means.

> —Philip Roth, *Writing American Fiction* (1961)

1

'My project', he told us, 'is to learn where to go by discovering where I am by reviewing where I've been—where we've all been. There's a kind of snail in the Maryland marshes—perhaps I invented him—that makes his shell as he goes along out of whatever he comes across, cementing it with his own juices, and at the same time makes his path instinctively toward the best available material for his shell; he carries his history on his back, living in it, adding new and larger spirals to it from the present as he grows. That snail's pace has become my pace—but I'm going in circles, following my own trail! I've quit reading and writing; I've lost track of who I am; my name's just a jumble of letters; so's the whole body of literature: strings of letters and empty spaces, like a code that I've lost the key to.'

—John Barth, *Chimera* (1972)

When we talk about the 'rise' or 'death' of literary genres, we are talking about status, mainly. The novel no longer has the supreme status it enjoyed for ninety years (1875–1965), but neither has the New Journalism won it for itself. The status of the New Journalism is not secured by any means. In some quarters the contempt for it is boundless . . . even breathtaking. . . . With any luck at all the new genre will never be sanctified, never be exalted, never given a theology. . . . All I meant to say when I started out was that the New Journalism can no longer be ignored in an artistic sense. The rest I take back. . . . The hell with it. . . . Let chaos reign . . . louder music, more wine. . . . The hell with the standings. . . . The top rung is up for grabs. All the old traditions are exhausted, and no new one is yet established. All bets are off! the odds are cancelled! it's anybody's ball game! . . . the horses are all drugged! the track is glass! . . . and out of such glorious chaos may come, from the most unexpected source, in the most unexpected form, some nice new fat Star Streamer Rockets that will light up the sky.

—Tom Wolfe, *The New Journalism* (1973)

Later I got out of Berkeley and went to New York and later I got out of New York and came to Los Angeles. What I have made for myself is personal, but is not exactly peace. Only one person I knew at Berkeley later discovered an ideology, dealt himself into history, cut himself loose from both his own dread and his own time. A few of the people I knew at Berkeley killed themselves not long after. Another attempted suicide in Mexico and then, in a recovery which seemed in many ways a more advanced derangement, came home and joined the Bank of America's three-year executive-training program. Most of us live less theatrically, but remain the survivors of a peculiar and inward time. If I could believe that going to a barricade would affect man's fate in the slightest I would go to that barricade, and quite often I wish that I could, but it would be less than honest to say that I expect to happen upon such a happy ending.

—Joan Didion, 'On the Morning after the Sixties' (1970)

The word 'new' seems endemic to American culture, surfacing constantly as an epithet to define the essential terms, and intentions, of the culture's beliefs and values. The 'new', as such, speaks not just to America's modern condition, nor just to its novel and distinctive place in history (a continuing mission to create a new society); but to its belief in continuing change. 'New' thus has about it a sense of American idealism, for it does not threaten the culture so much as speak to its most positive aspects: its optimism, pragmatism, and, of course, openness to the present and innovation. Harold Rosenberg's description of the United States as a 'tradition of the new' is, thus, both apposite and pertinent and gives precedence to a continuing belief in the radical. New is, thus, now.

And certainly one major tenet of the American literary tradition has always been fuelled by a belief that part of its destiny is to speak to and for the new. It is as fundamental to Whitman and Emerson as it is to William Carlos Williams and Dos Passos just as, in a more general context, it underpins so many other developments in American painting, photography, music, dance, film and, of course, architecture. Ezra Pound's dictum that the American artist must 'make it new' is pervasive; as much a part of the writer's perspective as is Whitman's declaration that he would 'strike up for a new world'.

The 1960s in particular seemed to take upon themselves this sense of the radical, and much of the literature from the period reflects an underlying (but misplaced) sense of

3

optimism based on what it was felt the times could create. The expansive rhetoric of John F. Kennedy offered a return to American idealism and a resurgence of American myth and possibility. As it moved away from the 'tranquilized fifties' so America, once again, seemed on the verge of yet another new beginning and new direction. In 1967, for example, Penguin Books published Donald Allen's and Robert Creeley's *The New Writing in the U.S.A.* (Allen had already edited his central *The New American Poetry*): an anthology of prose and poetry which reflected much of this sense of possibility and new-found impetus in a recharged and radical literature which found much of its imaginative energy from its use of American myth. What made it speak so directly to the times was what the editors saw as a 'shift' on the part of the writers,

> first, to their own places: the actual conditions of their lives; and second, westward—towards the West and the Pacific slopes of America, to the Orient, and southward to Central and South America.[1]

A cultural geography which, in its echoes of Whitman, saw in place an alternative reality: an ideal condition central to the culture's continuing sense of destiny and mission.

Such a perspective hardly seems possible from this point in the 1980s. Indeed one of the consistent concerns of the new writing since the '60s is the extent to which geography and the myth of American place has succumbed *to* history. Where it remains central is when 'place' is asked to yield a *lost* history: a separate cultural nexus to counter the times in which the ethnic writer finds him or her self. Indeed, one of the common characteristics of the writers considered in this volume is the way in which each is concerned *with* history: as condition, process, abstraction, fiction; as a force which increasingly seems to overwhelm and threaten. History bears down on the writing to at once question not just the validity of the 'self' but, in many instances, the very possibility of 'art' and of the 'word' to understand the world at all.

Watergate and Vietnam, of course, have for many compounded this sense of confusion and madness; but there is a larger, more pervasive atmosphere in much recent writing

4

which, as part of a larger historical condition, constantly qualifies any attempt to be 'new'. If in many ways the '70s and '80s have seen a retrenchment on the part of the writer, they have done so against a larger sense of things being at once more complex and disordered whilst equally seeming to be more predetermined and categorized. What Tony Tanner called, in his seminal study of post-war American fiction, *City of Words* (1971) part of an 'abiding American dread that someone else is patterning your life'[2] has increasingly been felt amidst a reality which itself seems meaningless and unknowable. What Philip Roth saw as the attempt to 'make credible' an American reality which 'stupefies' and 'sickens', and what Norman Podhoretz called 'the incredible reality of American life in the twentieth century', has seemingly become more incredible and more problematic.[3] It has become for many writers what Umberto Eco has called a 'furious hyperreality'[4]: a surreal otherness increasingly beyond any attempt to picture or understand the terms on which it exists.

Given such circumstances the American self does indeed seem under what Saul Bellow has called a 'great strain': a predicament according to Christopher Lasch where the self is 'overwhelmed by the cruelty, disorder, and sheer complexity of modern history'. In such circumstances the writer 'retreats into a solipsistic mode of discourse' and thus 'The only art that seems appropriate to such an age . . . is an anti-art or minimal art.'[5] If one response has been towards just such a minimalist aesthetic, in other writers the response has been the very opposite. The period, as we might expect, has been characterized by an insistent and continuing plurality of effort and of changing and unpredictable developments. Thus Tom Wolfe's claim in *The New Journalism* (1975) that this 'new' genre would 'wipe out the novel as literature's main event'[6] is as welcomingly contradicted by the publication of his own mammoth *The Bonfire of the Vanities* (1988) as is the sense that partial groupings and themes cannot match or do justice to the period's most obvious achievement: what has been called its 'insistent diversity of the ways in which experience can be organized in prose'.[7]

Certainly this has remained, rightly or wrongly, one of the

major distinctions between American and English writing over the same period. Bernard Bergonzi, for example, was adamant in his 1970 study *The Situation of the Novel* that there was a qualitative difference between the two literatures: the one (English) increasingly conservative and limited; the other (American) increasingly innotative and exploratory: open to the terms and conditions of the age in which it was written—a response on the part of the American writer which he defined as 'the constant probing of the relation between fiction and reality'.[8]

Indeed, in an anthology of American prose writing published nine years later in 1979, the *New American Writing* (*Granta*) Bergonzi's distinctions were reiterated with the fervour of fundamental belief. A collection which included pieces from John Hawkes, William Gass, Joyce Carol Oates, James Purdy, Donald Barthelme, Stanley Elkin and Ronald Sukenick was offered as exemplary evidence of American dominance and innovation. Thus 'today's British novel is neither remarkable nor remarkably interesting' but characterized by 'a steady, uninspired sameness, a predictable, even if articulate prattling of predictable predicaments'. As distinct from this the contemporary American writer has achieved 'some of the most challenging, diversified, and adventurous writing today.'[9] A distinction further emphasized by a second *Granta* anthology entitled *Dirty Realism: New Writing from America* (1983) where such figures as Raymond Carver, Jayne Anne Phillips and Elizabeth Tallent were viewed as part of a new fiction, of a 'peculiar and haunting kind':[10] yet another distinctive and 'new' American development.

It is against such a background that the following essays are offered. They are not concerned with the established talents who came to the fore in the immediate period following 1945 (Mailer, Salinger, Capote, Burroughs and Bellow, for example), nor with the 'second' generation of post-war writers who challenged and extended the writing of the '40s and '50s (Pynchon, Vonnegut, Brautigan and Hawkes, for example). Significantly not one of the writers considered is mentioned in *City of Words*, but all have created a literature notable for both its awareness of an American tradition and the demands of the time to be understood and perceived through a response appropriate to the 'new' age in which the writers find themselves.

The first five essays, then, offer assessments of writers who have extended and recast the concerns of the American writer. 'New writing' in this sense does not imply a radical break or technical innovation but a continuing attempt to make literature amidst what A. Alvarez termed 'a new kind of reality'. Thus five prose writers, E. L. Doctorow (the most established of the writers considered), Toni Morrison, Don DeLillo, Raymond Carver and Gordon Lish are each treated as individual talents responding in distinct and individual ways to this 'new reality'. While their work is seen as symptomatic of larger developments and concerns, they are, primarily, considered as individual figures for their individual effort. Two final essays suggest wider contexts in which to view some of the newer writing. The first, on recent developments in American ethnic writing, considers the significance of Chicano, American Indian and American Chinese writing and how their resurgence at once extends and complicates the map of American ethnic writing; the second, on recent American detective and crime fiction, suggests the ways in which a traditional American genre has developed in radical and distinctive ways in response to a world bounded by the realities and moral ambiguities created by such major historical events as Vietnam and Watergate.

Taken as a whole the essays speak to what can only be a small part of an ever-increasing plurality and complexity of response on the part of American writers: what has recently been called the 'embarrassment of riches' of the contemporary American offering; a body of work which consistently 'defies easy reduction to tendencies and trends'.[11] Perhaps above all what the writers here considered speak to is precisely that continuing belief in the capacity of the written word to make sense of an impossible world and an impossible situation. Their attempts to confront the implications of their historical circumstances, for all their differences of belief and subject-matter, thus share a common basis and compulsion. Their writing speaks to what, in his analysis of DeLillo, Eric Mottram calls the 'real needs' of man; not just to 'make it new', but to confront the new in distinctive terms, appropriate to the times in which they live.

NOTES

1. Donald Allen and Robert Creeley (eds.), *The New Writing in the U.S.A.* (Harmondsworth: Penguin, 1967), p. 10. Allen's *The New American Poetry* was published in 1960 (New York: Grove Press). *The New Writing in the U.S.A.* includes Brautigan, Burroughs, Creeley, Ginsberg, Jones, Kerouac, Olson, Sorrentino and Zukofsky.
2. Tony Tanner, *City of Words: A Study of American Fiction in the Mid-Twentieth Century* (London: Jonathan Cape, 1971), p. 15.
3. See Philip Roth, 'Writing American Fiction' in *Reading Myself and Others* (London: Corgi, 1977), pp. 107–25. The essay was first published in 1961. See also Norman Podhoretz, *Doings and Undoings* (1964).
4. Umberto Eco, *Travels in Hyperreality* (London: Picador, 1987), trans. William Weaver. See especially Eco's brilliant chapter 'Travels in Hyperreality', pp. 1–58.
5. Christopher Lasch, *The Minimal Self: Psychic Survival in Troubled Times* (London: Picador, 1985), Section IV: 'The Minimalist Aesthetic', pp. 130–62. The quotation is from page 131.
6. Tom Wolfe and E. W. Johnson (eds.), *The New Journalism* (London: Picador, 1975), p. 22.
7. *New American Writing, Granta* (Autumn, 1979), 5.
8. Bernard Bergonzi, *The Situation of the Novel* (1970, Harmondsworth: Penguin, 1972), p. 114. But see especially Chapters 3 and 4.
9. *New American Writing*, pp. 3–5.
10. *Dirty Realism: New Writing from America, Granta*, No. 8, 4–5.
11. Eugene Goodheart, 'Four Decades of Contemporary American Fiction' in Vol. 9, *American Literature*, of *The New Pelican Guide to English Literature*, ed. Boris Ford (Harmondsworth: Penguin, 1988), pp. 617–37.

1

Writing on the Margin: E. L. Doctorow and American History

by HENRY CLARIDGE

1

It is an accepted part of the 'conventional wisdom' about the American novel that it has largely eschewed history and society in preference for existential and metaphysical speculation. Alexis de Tocqueville predicted as much in *Democracy in America* (1835, 1840) and much post-war criticism of the American novel has tended to find evidence for his thesis. In *The American Adam* (1955), for example, R. W. B. Lewis proposed that at the epicentre of the American myth was

> an individual emancipated from history, happily bereft of ancestry, untouched and undefiled by the usual inheritance of family and race; an individual standing alone, self-reliant and self-propelling, ready to confront whatever awaited him with the aid of his own unique and inherent resources.[1]

Some five years later Leslie Fielder in *Love and Death in the American Novel* gave this individual a sexual life, but the essential features of an a-historical culture remained intact. Throughout the 1960s this view of the American novel more or less held sway, but it took on the colourings of a different vocabulary: in his synoptic account of post-war American fiction, *Radical Innocence* (1961), Ihab Hassan spoke in the

9

existential language of freedom and self-definition for those anti-heroes who occupy centre-stage in most contemporary American novels; in *Beyond the Waste Land: The American Novel in the Nineteen-Sixties* (1972) Raymond M. Olderman gave the fiction of the period a configuration and character that owes much to myth criticism, arguing that the novel of the 1960s deserts realism and its attendant problems for the romance form with its freedom from fidelity and its gravitation towards the 'fabulous nature of fact'.[2]

Critics, of course, can often be accused of selecting those works which fit their *weltanschaung*, but the view of the American novel as an essentially a-historical and a social phenomenon, offered initially to account for the 'classic' phase of American Literature but subsequently extended into the fiction of the 1960s, was receiving powerful reinforcement from the practitioners themselves, notably from Philip Roth who, in his 1960 Stanford University speech, spoke of the American writer in the middle of the twentieth century as having

> his hands full in trying to understand, describe, and then make *credible* much of American reality. It stupefies, it sickens, it infuriates, and finally it is even a kind of embarrassment to one's meagre imagination. The actuality is continually outdoing our talents, and the culture tosses up figures almost daily that are the envy of any novelist.[3]

Roth, in other words, offers good reasons for the writer's retreat from the 'actual' into the freer latitudes of the romance or the fantastic. Something of the same kind of disavowal of objective reality is at work in Norman Mailer's notion of 'factoids' or in the increasingly phantasmagoric, allegoric and satirical strain that surfaced in black fiction in the late 1960s, notably in the writings of Imamu Amiri Baraka (LeRoi Jones), Sam Greenlees, Ishmael Reed and John A. Williams.

Obviously a more elastic definition of realism can be used to accommodate the various forms of experimentation, both with narrative and subject-matter, that characterize the American post-modernist novel of the past two or tree decades. An account of realism that emphasizes the interaction between the individual and society at the expense of, or the increasing exclusion of, the subjectivity of the author (something, in other words, like the notion of 'classic realism' in contemporary critical theory) will not adequately describe the fiction of John Barth or John Hawkes or John Irving, but one that can embrace the subjectivity of the author and his or her denial of the 'significance' of 'daily life' might satisfactorily include the differing 'realities' that emerge from introspective and autobiographical modes of fiction. It is hard to establish the extent to which contemporary criticism of the American novel may have buttressed developments and changes in the American novel itself, but much recent criticism of the American novel has tended to promote a less exclusive definition of literary realism and the novel itself has presented strong evidence in support of the definition.

All this is by way of 'placing' the fiction of E. L. Doctorow in both that larger history of the American novel which takes us back to Cooper, Hawthorne and Melville, and that more immediate history which includes contemporaries such as Hawkes, Roth and Updike. Doctorow's relationship to his contemporaries is both curious and ambiguous: he has been, particularly in recent years, an extremely successful novelist (he turned to writing as a career, it might be noted, in 1969) and this might necessarily exclude him from a place amongst the avant-garde; at the same time, he has experimented with narrative voice and narrative method in ways which give his fiction certain first-order difficulties. Moreover, the experimentation has been in two senses backward-looking: Doctorow's materials are those of American history, particularly that phase from the 1900s to the late 1960s, and his forms show a striking resemblance to those of the American historical romance.[4] For Doctorow the 'self-reliant and self-propelling' individual of whom R. W. B. Lewis spoke is not a plausible subject, since for him identity is a socially and historically constructed concept, not one immune from historical determinism. His characters, in other words, are treated as historically determined (no differently, it might be noted, from the characters one meets in the great realist novels of the nineteenth century), yet the narrative pattern against which their histories are played out wilfully fractures

11

the stability and order that comes from chronological and temporal progression and places them in an essentially indeterminate and elusive historical space.

Although Doctorow is very much 'our contemporary' it is salutary to remind ourselves that his first novel, *Welcome to Hard Times,*[5] was published in 1960. It was followed by *Big as Life* (1964), a novel Doctorow has effectively disowned and which he has blocked against subsequent reprinting. After this there was an hiatus of seven years before the appearance of *The Book of Daniel* (1971), and one can surmise that it was the critical and commercial success of this novel which gave rise to that productive phase of the past decade and a half which includes *Ragtime* (1975), *Loon Lake* (1980), *Lives of the Poets* (1984), *World's Fair* (1985), and, most recently, *Billy Bathgate* (1989), as well as the play, *Drinks Before Dinner* (1979).

Taken as a whole the novels (*Lives of the Poets* is a collection of loosely connected short stories and a novella) constitute an imaginative revision of American history from the closing of one frontier, the real frontier of the American West, to that of another frontier, the idealized frontier of the Great Society programmes (and its attendant mythology) at the end of the 1960s. For all the various experiments with voice that Doctorow effects, the signature these texts carry is that of a liberal-left American, the product of a lower middle-class, Jewish, socialist-leaning, Bronx family. The natural scepticism such people have traditionally had to the more extreme claims of the American dream (though they often, of course, manifest it) was powerfully reinforced by the Depression (Doctorow was born at its beginning in 1931). The older products of this kind of environment, writers like Abraham Cahan and Henry Roth, were drawn to political commitment and philosophical scepticism; Doctorow seems to have replaced the latter with historical scepticism, particularly with regard to the 'received' history of the United States in the twentieth century. He has sought a fictional form that can accommodate a revisionist and imaginative history of modern America, one that can unpack the mythology of American life and at the same time encompass the moral fate of the American people.[6]

These are large, one might say, grandiose demands and

they seem to presuppose an almost Tolstoyan magnitude; but Doctorow like any novelist has been constrained by the ineluctable individualism of the novel form, its besetting concern with individual lives and individual cases. The constraints are especially visible in his first novel of the post-1970 period, *The Book of Daniel*. Here Doctorow's subject was, as he himself explained in an interview, 'the story of the American left in general and the generally sacrificial rôle it has played in our history'.[7] One could be forgiven for thinking that such a statement describes the subject of an historical study or the proposal for a doctoral dissertation, rather than a work of fiction, but Doctorow has clearly always seen his writing originating in some aspect or moment of historical change which is then subjected to imaginative re-creation. In *The Book of Daniel* the 'story of the American left' narrows to the 'story' of Julius and Ethel Rosenberg, executed on 19 June 1953 for espionage (particularly the passing of top secret information to the Soviet Union, including details of the atomic bomb). Doctorow is not interested in the case history as such (which for him is another *kind* of narrative or fiction), but in the resonances of the Rosenberg case as it is viewed from the hindsight accorded to it by the events of the late 1960s. Doctorow's historical scepticism, of course, tells him that the events of the 1960s do not inhabit some objective, verifiable historical world, but belong to the anecdotal and the autobiographical. We know from his interviews that he began *The Book of Daniel* in the third person, found the voice boring, and was in despair at his failure to imaginatively realize such a momentous subject. The shift to a more fluid medium, where Daniel Isaacson's (the weakly disguised invented name for the imagined son of the real life Rosenbergs) voice interacts with that of an ostensibly third-person narrator, successfully fractures and subverts the expected chronology of events, forcing the reader to see that the history of the executed spies is, literally, 'the book of Daniel', that account of it, autobiographical and subjective, offered by a son and subject to the vagaries of impression and memory.

Behind Doctorow's wilful obliquity there is, of course, an intellectual and argumentative paradox. While *The Book*

13

of Daniel retreats from the question of the Rosenberg's guilt or innocence (it is, after all, a work of fiction and thus *could* make the Isaacsons guilty or innocent, but cannot by extrapolation apportion guilt or innocence to the Rosenbergs), it does make historical claims: it invites the reader to accept that Daniel's story is more real and palpable than any straight-historical narrative and thus, implicitly, privileges this account above all others; we are invited, in other words, to treat this as the 'real' history.

The constraints of which I spoke earlier are those which demand that the novelist tells a story with individualized characters whose destinies concern and often, emotionally, affect us. In addition, Doctorow is constrained by the demands that his concern with history places on him; he cannot, after all, simply make things up (in part a good reason for thinking him a realist), nor is he content with the historical past as it is passed down to him through the 'received' histories. His recent expressions of his great interest in oral history and the sometimes striking similarities his books have with notable works of oral history (I am thinking particularly of the profitable comparison that can be made between Studs Terkel's *Hard Times* (1970) and Doctorow's *Loon Lake*) is indicative of the new social historian *manqué* one often discovers when reading him. Oral history, it seems, has for Doctorow the strength that comes from 'felt' experience and is free of the mediating control of an author with a particular thesis or 'version' of the past; in addition, the historical witness addresses the reader with the freedom of idiom and the conversational voice that authenticates the experiences recorded. Finding a way of using this mode has, I think, been at the centre of Doctorow's technical innovations over the past decade.

It is in *Ragtime* (1975) that Doctorow's relationship with American history and the fictional problems of recasting history become more salient and significant. Where *The Book of Daniel* had, in a sense, re-imagined historical figures and given them new fictional identities, *Ragtime* circumvents the fictionalizing process by using real historical figures in the imagined context of the novel where they play out their destinies alongside those 'complex predicates' of

14

the author's imagination. There is, of course, nothing new about this: in Tolstoy's *War and Peace* Napoleon and General Kutuzov are 'characters' in the fiction and are given words, speeches·and motives which belong not to history (though Tolstoy always insisted on his fidelity to the historical record) but to the imagination. In *Ragtime* the Jewish radical Emma Goldman inhabits the story of Coalhouse Walker, a ragtime pianist and, later, black revolutionary, and his wife, Sarah. Coalhouse, driven by racism to radical action, steals the art treasury of the real J. P. Morgan and threatens to destroy it. His 'conversion' to political radicalism is dramatized against a sharply realized and re-created background of those debates about the black cause, between integrationists and separatists, that surfaced in the United States in the early years of this century. After the death of Sarah (she is mistaken by the police for an assassin, hit in the chest by the butt of a rifle, and dies later from pneumonia) Coalhouse leads a gang of like-minded black Americans on various terrorist missions, and, in an attempt to divert him from his senseless path, is visited in J. P. Morgan's library by the 'real' Booker T. Washington. Thus Doctorow constructs the confrontation of the real and the imagined as a dramatized moment in the history of competing black ideologies.

As this account of part of Coalhouse Walker's story should suggest, Doctorow is attempting to give his fiction historical authenticity by obscuring (and complicating) the relationship an imaginary character has with his 'real' background, since the background here is not simply some geographically locatable place (in this case, New York) but also historical personages taken from it and made into fictional characters. Doctorow is, therefore, in part, constrained by known historical events and is not free to re-invent the past in some way that makes it peculiarly accessible to his fictional concerns. On the other hand, by treating historical personages as characters in his work he is given a certain amount of freedom to improvise 'historical' events around them, and in *Ragtime* he does this with a good deal of *brio*. But this is fraught with danger: the reader may take a particular pleasure in the conclusion of *Ragtime* when, after Coalhouse's surrender, Younger Brother drives the band's Model T Ford off to

Mexico to find the revolutionary leader Emiliano Zapata, while we are simultaneously reminded of Woodrow Wilson's election, J. P. Morgan's European tour, the assassination of the Archduke Ferdinand in Sarajevo, and a spectacular feat by Harry Houdini in Times Square, all compressed into a conclusion in which we are told that 'the era of Ragtime had run out'.[8] The pleasure is mitigated, however, by our sense of Doctorow's pushing of things towards the whimsical, and when Sigmund Freud travels through an amusement park 'Tunnel of Love' with Carl Jung this reinforces our sense that the playfulness can quite easily backfire; we are not so much dazzled by Doctorow's technique, as Paul Levine argues,[9] as irritated and slightly embarrassed. Whether this trip occurred or not is beside the point (Freud and Jung visited Coney Island during their American tour in September 1909): the detail serves no purpose, it provides no more than a spurious historicity which directs our attention towards the clever, rather than intelligent, author.

A number of commentators have suggested the possible comparison of *Ragtime* with John Dos Passos's *U.S.A.* (1938), but the comparison is not a particularly productive one, largely because *U.S.A.* (by which I mean the completed trilogy) is so much the more ambitious work, and, in part, because Doctorow and Dos Passos take such differing attitudes to the dramatization of the historical past. But the two novels are similar in their attempts to treat of more than one character's story (in *U.S.A.* it is a multiple of stories) and to render something of the density of American social experience. The story of Coalhouse Walker which I described above is held 'inside' another story, that of Tateh, a socialist Jewish immigrant who goes from silhouette artist to film-maker, and whose upwardly mobile life (away from working-class radicalism towards the American dream) provides a check and a foil to Coalhouse's bleaker tale. Tateh's story (and that of other Jewish immigrants like him) is, one might reasonably surmise, the autobiographical tale, the closest approximation to the 'camera eye' sections that punctuate *U.S.A.* And one might think, therefore, that it provides the strategic route whereby Doctorow can escape from the text by offering competing, and thus neutralizing, versions of the American experience. This, however, is not the case. *Ragtime* is quite merciless in its indictments of American life, and these often verge on, if not fall into, the sentimental and the romantic, notably in the treatment of Coalhouse Walker and Mother, and in the way we are invited to wallow in the ultimately bogus revolutionary zeal of the novel, siding with the 'oppressed' while we luxuriate in Doctorow's re-creation of the cars, clothes, furnishings, and *mores* of an unregenerate capitalist age.

Ragtime was the critical and commercial success of the year on its appearance in the United States, winning the National Book Critics' Circle Award for 1976 and marginally coming in first as best-selling hardback novel of the book year (the film rights were subsequently sold for $2,000,000). It is, however, by no means Doctorow's best novel and should be seen, essentially, as a developmental point in his progress as a writer of fiction. In it Doctorow finds a way of taking hold of a rich historical period and dramatizing it through a host of background characters (some real, some invented) who give us a sense of society in action. What he does not adequately resolve is the relationship between the historical and the fictional materials, of which the use of real historical personages is the most visible exemplification. It is this relationship which is addressed again in the later novels, *Loon Lake* and *World's Fair*.

2

Other than some minor pieces of non-fiction (some political, some autobiographical reflections on the rôle of the writer) Doctorow published nothing after *Ragtime* for four years. 1979 saw the appearance of the play *Drinks Before Dinner*, an interesting exercise in the imaginative voicing of what appear to be allegorical parts, but an unequivocal failure as a dramatic work, though Doctorow in his introduction to the script tries to forestall this obvious criticism.[10] The play's interest, for any student of Doctorow, lies in its place as a kind of 'first-run' of *Loon Lake*, the novel which appeared, uncharacteristically for Doctorow, almost immediately after the play. The contrasts between the two works are legion, the play contemporary and concerned with middle-class characters, the novel historical and dealing with the marginalized poor and unemployed of the Great Depression, but the techniques are markedly similar with *Loon Lake* putting its characters before us in 'disynchronous' (Doctorow's word), first- and third-person forms made more perplexing by shifts (seemingly random) in time and space. The technique makes *Loon Lake* a 'difficult' work for the reader, and Doctorow is to be commended for not following the commercial route offered by the success of *Ragtime* and resting his talents on its essentially formulaic nature.

Loon Lake gives further, and arguably, stronger, evidence for the description of Doctorow as 'the novelist as revisionist historian' with his impulse to restore 'lost' groups to the historical record. Like the earlier novel it is an attempt to tell a series of stories, initially discontinuous with one another, which in themselves enact a vertical history of the United States in the year 1936, though contextual information is provided backwards and forwards from this date. The central characters through whom this world is reconstructed are: Joe (christened, we learn at the end, Joseph Korzeniowski, the 'real' name of Joseph Conrad), a young man from Paterson, New Jersey, who becomes one of the innumerable hobos of the Depression years; Warren Penfield, a poet from Indianapolis, born at the turn of the century, who serves in the Great War and dies mysteriously in 1937; and F. W. Bennett, a multi-millionaire industrial overlord, whose mansion at Loon Lake in the Adirondack mountains (in upstate New York) acts as a kind of centripetal draw on the various destinies which inhabit the novel. Doctorow is here reworking something of the tripartite structure we saw him using in *Ragtime*, setting Joe and Warren as countervailing forces in the novel (like Coalhouse and Tateh in *Ragtime*) with Bennett filling the rôle assigned earlier to J. P. Morgan. These individuals are, in part, devices to enable him to dramatize his version of American history and, in turn, fill out the necessary human and social context. By presenting society as a complex web of individual relationships, Doctorow overcomes the problems often set for the historical novel by the tendency towards the generalized and the abstract which one sees in novels with either a vast historical canvas or a vast canvas of characters (for example, Steinbeck's *The Grapes of Wrath* (1939), where the intercalary chapters are hopelessly abstract and externalized).

Much of the world of *Loon Lake* is presented through what one might call a fictional form of oral history, using the various voices, particularly that of Joe, to provide an anecdotal and autobiographical historical document, not a verifiable and objective one. Doctorow, as I remarked earlier, seems to be conversant with the rich body of autobiographical reminiscence of the Depression years and Joe's voicing of his story (Doctorow aims at a conversational and spoken idiom for him which is often masterful) echoes the voices of some of those interviewed for the 'Hard Travelin'' section of Terkel's *Hard Times: An Oral History of the Great Depression.*

> I got along with all the freaks, I made a point to. It was as if I had to acclimate myself to the worst there was. I never let them see that I had any special awareness of them. I knew it was important not to act like a rube. After a while they stopped looking at me with the carney eyes and forgot I was there.[11]

(Thus Joe describing the freaks with whom he works on an itinerant carnival.) But while he adequately renders the flatly descriptive nuances we would expect of Joe, Doctorow also gives him poetic and literary qualities, an effect we can compare with that balance of the naturalistic and poetic that Twain achieves with Huckleberry Finn or Faulkner with Dewey Dell in *As I Lay Dying* (1930). Thus the opening words of the novel, 'They were hateful presences in me' (p. 7), Joe describing his parents, or the following account Joe gives of being bitten by dogs on Bennett's estate—

> Somehow I was vaulted or inspired upward in some acrobatic backward tumble through the unframed shack window. I took one of the dogs with me, slamming it fixed in my wrist against the inner wall of the shack while the heads of the others appeared outside the window, a fountain of faces leaping and falling back in rage and frustration. (p. 46)

—belong to the internal, poetic voice rather than that which we would naturalistically expect of him. Yet Doctorow is aware that this voice, whether naturalistic or poetic, is insufficient for the whole work (and, probably, unsustainable), so it is interrupted by another voice, discontinuous with it and not authorial, but in effect 'speaking itself' and providing at first poetical invention and subsequently narrative detail. This 'interrupting' voice is presented in what looks like 'computerese', computer data which composes a life in factual information, and this voice, in turn, is interrupted by what looks ostensibly like third-person narration.

Increasingly, as we plunge deeper into the world of *Loon Lake*, the novel becomes more like a montage, or what another critic has called a 'bricolage'.[12] The shifts of point of view, the interweaving of differing languages, styles and registers of speech, produce a deliberately destabilizing effect on the reader which Doctorow has argued produces few problems for anyone familiar with the techniques and conventions of narrative film. It is also, I surmise, evidence of Doctorow's familiarity with contemporary narrative theory with its emphasis on the polysemantic nature of the written text and its appeal to the re-creating and defamiliarizing processes given such importance in the act of writing in post-modernist fiction. The difficulty, however, raised by the wilful use of these fracturing and fragmenting techniques is that they may work at the expense of the subject-matter, and for a writer like Doctorow, keen of dealing with the 'real' and on unpacking the obfuscations of history, there may be an unhappy marriage of methods and materials. Joe's voice with its attentiveness to detail and its rich particularity helps to overcome this, and despite his rags-to-riches story (two other characters in the novel, Penfield and Clara, Bennett's mistress, also enact this escape from working-class upbringings) Joe is used by Doctorow, particularly in the opening chapters of the novel, as the voice of moral commentary on the acquisitive capitalist world (as he sees it) of Sim Hearn's carnival and the insulated mansion of F. W. Bennett. It is this world of which Joe is initially the critic that finally seduces and absorbs him with its connected attractions of power and status.

While *Loon Lake* to my mind is a qualified success (it is, on a second reading, a more satisfying and rewarding book than *Ragtime*), the vertiginous effects wrought by the shifts of narrative voice and genre produce an initially bewildering experience for the reader, and given Doctorow's relentless experimentation with form we are not surprised to find that his two subsequent works are presented in a very different register. I want to leave *Lives of the Poets* (1985) to my conclusion, both for reasons of its form and its materials. In *World's Fair* (1986) Doctorow has moved the date on three years from that of *Loon Lake* to 1939 and the New York World's Fair, but the retrospective element of the novel takes us back through the early 1930s to the First World War in a loving re-creation of the sights, sounds and smells of a Bronx childhood. Throughout the novel is in the first person, but the voice varies. At the beginning it is that of Rose, the mother, in the later stages of the book it is the two sons, Donald and Edgar, the last name not seeking to disguise the fact that we are reading an autobiographical voice; Donald's and Rose's sections are marked, as is one by Aunt Frances, while the remainder of the novel is in Edgar's voice. In its presentation of different points of view without the presence of any intervening or mediating authorial voice the novel has affinities with Faulkner's *As I Lay Dying*. What is also worth noting, moreover, is how so much of the first-person mode continues that experimentation with the oral historical form that I noted in *Loon Lake*.

There can be no doubt that *World's Fair* is more accessible to the reader than the earlier work, in great part because of the temporal linearity of the novel. There can also be no doubt that Doctorow, like so many other American writers, is very much at home in the autobiographical medium, and while this medium is by its very nature introspective and self-regarding, it is also available to Doctorow's particular kind of historical inquiry, for it is a way of connecting one's present circumstances with those past experiences, familial and social, which gave rise to them. We need Rose's voice here, not so much as a way of providing a perspective on her sons (she speaks her sections as if *to* them), but more as a way of enlarging and deepening our sense of the social and historical world the family inhabits. In *World's Fair*, in other words, Doctorow makes the novel over into a form of oral history.

The inevitable consequence of this move towards the autobiographical is that Doctorow is forced to dispense with what he would see as the fictional contrivances of plot and story, and has to rely on his ability to create a picture of the world the family inhabits. With Edgar he goes back to experiences of which the boy, presumably, would have only the most indistinct memory but which are presented with great directness:

> Startled awake by the ammoniated mists, I am roused in one instant from glutinous sleep to grieving awareness; I have done it again. My soaked thighs sting. I cry, I call Mama, knowing I must endure her harsh reaction, get through *that*, to be rescued. My crib is on the east wall of their room. Their bed is on the south wall. 'Mama!' From her bed she hushes me. 'Mama!' She groans, rises, advances on me in her white nightgown.[13]

What Doctorow records is the birth of a subject slowly taking possession of the world around him, first the room in which he sleeps and the parents he occasionally sleeps with, later his brother and the family dog, then his Grandmother, and by a series of extensions of the boy's enlarging consciousness, his street, his neighbourhood, his city, and finally the world itself, symbolized in the World's Fair, which in a striking historical paradox comes in 1939 to image a prosperous and stable future precisely at that moment when, in Europe, war comes to dampen such innocent hopes:

> And then the amazing thing was that at the end you saw a particular model street intersection and the show was over, and with your I HAVE SEEN THE FUTURE button in your hand you came out into the sun and you were standing on precisely the corner you had just seen, the future was right where you were standing and what was small had become big, the scale had enlarged and you were no longer looking down at it, but standing in it, on this corner of the future, right here in the World's Fair! (p. 241)

All this is done with the memorizing voice, unlike that James Joyce uses at the beginning of *A Portrait of the Artist as a Young Man* (1916) which re-creates and replicates the consciousness of an infant; Doctorow's method deliberately dispels the objective, mimetic effect of the child's first person—

> In my own consciousness I was not a child. When I was alone, not subject to the demands of the world, I had the opportunity to be the aware sentient being I knew myself to be. (p. 19)

—thus challenging the separation of child from adult, by seeing the former as merely a coercive construction by the latter. This kind of psychological sophistication and complexity makes Doctorow's epigraph from Wordsworth's *The Prelude* less casual than it might initially appear. The lines, 'A raree-show is here, / With children gathered round . . . , from Book VII of *The Prelude* refer to the peep-shows, or shows in a box, that Wordsworth saw in the streets of London, and while Doctorow's reference is on one level to the idea of the World's Fair as a kind of show, of the world in miniature, it also carries the suggestion of the autobiographical eye/I as a 'peeping' out on to the world. Wordsworth's subtitle, of course, carries even deeper resonances which Doctorow is keen to pursue: *The Growth of a Poet's Mind* insists on us the degree to which the introspective, self-examining account takes precedence over the record of witness to external events. While *World's Fair* gives us a richly detailed picture of a New York, Jewish childhood in the 1930s and is, at times, a kind of imaginative guidebook to the texture of the period, it is even more so an act of introspective memorializing which comes close to, but happily never falls into, outright confession.

From *The Book of Daniel* in 1971 to *World's Fair* in 1986 there has been a development in Doctorow's fiction which can be seen as an inversion of his earlier premises. *The Book of Daniel* takes hold of historical events, re-imagines them, and introspects them through the eyes and thoughts of its eponymous hero. *Ragtime* in part does the same for a different historical period, but extends the method of fiction by drawing history and historical figures into the fictional world by making them co-extensive with the author's imaginings. *Loon Lake* maintains the contract with historical subjects but presents the past in a discontinuous, fragmented medium which suggests that Doctorow is becoming more interested in the techniques of story-telling than the materials of story-telling, but it remains, as I have argued, a more than qualified success. With *World's Fair* (it remains to be seen what Doctorow has done in *Billy Bathgate**) the first-person mode is used throughout the novel, and the shift to the autobiographical this brings finds Doctorow replacing the self-examining voice of Daniel with his own. All this, however, is prefigured in *Lives of the Poets* (1985), the collection of six short stories and a novella which preceded *World's Fair* and which Doctorow announced as having a direct connection with the novel that was to follow. The connection, of course, is the autobiographical one. *Lives of the Poets* draws on Doctorow's sojourn in a Greenwich village studio apartment at that point in his career when the success of *Ragtime* had catapulted him into the world of the literary celebrity. The novella which concludes the volume (it carries the title 'Lives of the Poets') is transparently autobiographical, recording the frustration, difficulties and inner turmoils of Jonathan, our writer and first-person witness:

> After you're married for several years you start waiting, and you don't even realize it, you become alert to something at the edge of the forest, you look up from your grazing and it isn't even there, the delicate sense behind all events all occasions of putting in time, making, killing time. Isn't that so, compadre? I mean bear with me even though you think I'm taking strength from numbers: You notice younger men than you going off stunningly from coronaries, embolisms, aneurysms, sudden cancerous devastations, every manner of swift scything, the achievement of their lives still to come. From one moment to the next, all that feisty character is plaintive, all that intention and high design has turned to pathos, and the custom-tailored suits are spectres in the closet. And what they did, these raucous smartass go-getters, turns out to be shamefully modest, of little consequence, they were their own greatest publicists and all the shouting was their own. So my discovery at fifty is that this mortal rush to solitude is pandemic, that is the news I bring.[14]

E. L. Doctorow and American History

These kinds of reflections are commingled in the story with observations and pictures of the life beyond Jonathan's apartment, presented not in any coherent pattern but randomly, as they might occur in life, so that the whole, while perfectly intelligible, reads like a stream of consciousness. Some of Jonathan's remarks, moreover, echo that despair of the American condition one finds in other contemporary Jewish writers, notably Saul Bellow. The comments, for example, on the new patterns of immigration to the United States, particularly that from Latin and Central America, are suffused with the sense of political and moral instability these new immigrants bring, but Doctorow's condemnation of American values remains unequivocal:

> Dear God, let them migrate, let my country be the last best hope. But let us make some distinctions here: The Irish, the Italians the Jews of Eastern Europe, came here because they wanted a new life. They worked for the money to bring over their families. They said good riddance to the old country and were glad to be gone. They did not come here because of something we had done to them. The new immigrants are here because we have made their lands unlivable. They have come here to save themselves from us. They have brought their hot politics with them. (p. 131)

Though we can question the truthfulness of what Jonathan says we cannot question, or impugn, the moral force of it. Indeed, Doctorow seems to have found in the autobiographical voice an instrument for his moral and political commentary that is so much more eloquent and authentic than that strident, but ultimately disingenuous, narrative voice which irredeemably weakens *The Book of Daniel* and *Ragtime*. But the success of the autobiographical voice is not unqualified, and 'Lives of the Poets' often takes on an exaggerated, over-insistent tone. It is in the earlier stories, particularly 'The Writer in the Family', 'The Water Works', and 'The Hunter', that the real strengths of the collection are to be found, and they contain, arguably, the best writing Doctorow has yet done. Ironically, the strength of these tales lies not in the style we have come to associate with Doctorow—demythologizing, politically committed, inventive,

25

sometimes whimsically so, in its use of historical materials—but in a style that is leaner, sparer, elliptical and emphatically within that great tradition of American story-telling one associates with Crane, Anderson and Hemingway, and contemporaries of Doctorow such as Brautigan and Carver. One senses it as much in *World's Fair* as here, and it offers powerful evidence that Doctorow is at his best, like so many other writers, when he ignores his manifesto.

3

In a chapter of her recent study of the American historical romance, Emily Miller Budick has argued that in Ragtime Doctorow has confirmed American fiction's 'continuing commitment to exploring the undecidability of literary meaning and to placing that indeterminacy within the claims of history.'[15] She charts the kinship, as she sees it, that *Ragtime* has with nineteenth-century works such as Cooper's *The Spy*, Hawthorne's *The House of the Seven Gables*, and Melville's *Billy Budd*, works which are finally sceptical about the nature of the reality and history they confront. It is the historical tendency in the classic American novel which contemporary critics of the American novel have been keen to discover, both as a revision and a correction of that view of the American novel, exemplified by Lewis and Fiedler, with which I opened this essay, and as a measurement of their commitment to the novel as an instrument of social and moral commentary and analysis. Doctorow's 'rediscovery' of American history as a subject, especially that excluded and marginalized part of it about which he writes, makes him peculiarly susceptible to this kind of criticism where the critic looks to the imaginative writer to confirm his or her moral and political positions. Doctorow, like so many writers, is taken over by his critics, and by instantaneous extrapolation one work comes to stand for the whole *oeuvre*. It is a superficially attractive view of him, but, as I have tried to show in this essay on his development as a writer from *The Book of Daniel* to the present, it is by no means adequate to what Doctorow has given to us. He has not remained static: the vertiginous effects of *Loon Lake* might have suggested that he was going to have even greater recourse to a technique of narrative fragmentation, only for us to find that his subsequent two works have found him drawing on the simple and the personal. Like so many of 'our contemporaries' he is still writing, and one can only speculate as to what his particular hybridization of the historical, the autobiographical and the post-modern will produce next. One thing is certain: it will not be what we expect, nor will it be what we have already read.

NOTES

1. R. W. B. Lewis, *The American Adam: Innocence, Tragedy and Tradition in the Nineteenth Century* (Chicago: University of Chicago Press, 1955), p. 5.
2. Raymond M. Olderman, *Beyond the Waste Land: The American Novel in the Nineteen-Sixties* (New Haven: Yale University Press, 1972), p. 5.
3. Philip Roth, *Reading Myself and Others* (Harmondsworth: Penguin Books, 1985), p. 176.
4. For a recent analysis of this form in American fiction see Emily Miller Budick, *Fiction and Historical Consciousness: The American Romance Tradition* (New Haven: Yale University Press, 1989).
5. Published in England as *The Bad Man from Bodie* (London: André Deutsch, 1961).
6. See Richard Trenner (ed.), *E. L. Doctorow: Essays and Conversations* (Princeton: Ontario Review Press, 1983), pp. 31–47.
7. Ibid., p. 61
8. E. L. Doctorow, *Ragtime* (London: Picador, 1985), p. 236.
9. Paul Levine, *E. L. Doctorow* (London: Methuen, 1985), p. 53. Levine's book is the best short introduction to Doctorow and it carries a useful bibliography.
10. E. L. Doctorow, *Drinks Before Dinner* (New York: Random House, 1979), p. xvi.
11. E. L. Doctorow, *Loon Lake* (London: Picador, 1985), p. 22. Subsequent references to this novel are given in parentheses in the text. The title, the name of a lake, refers to the loons, aquatic birds, found in upstate New York, and also, perhaps, to the sixteenth-century meaning of the word, 'rogue' or 'scamp', to describe the picaresque hero, Joe.
12. See Geoffrey Galt Harpham, 'E. L. Doctorow and the Technology of Narrative', *PMLA*, 100 (January 1985), 81–95.
13. E. L. Doctorow, *World's Fair* (London: Picador, 1987), p. 6. Subsequent references to this novel are given in parentheses in the text.

14. E. L. Doctorow, *Lives of the Poets* (London: Picador, 1986), p. 89. Subsequent references to this collection are given in parentheses in the text. The title is, again, of interest referring as it does to Samuel Johnson's *Lives of the Poets* which Doctorow's volume in no way resembles.
15. Budick, p. 186.

*Postscript

The article above was written before the publication of *Billy Bathgate* in Great Britain. The novel's appearance here now gives me the opportunity to offer some remarks about it. What is instantly noticeable is how that shift in style and method I observed in Doctorow's more recent works (especially *Lives of the Poets* and *World's Fair*) is confirmed in this latest novel. *Billy Bathgate* is told through the eyes and voice of its eponymous hero, its setting New York, and particularly the Bronx of Billy's childhood, its subject the infamous Dutch Schultz gang for which Billy Bathgate (his surname taken from that of a Bronx street) becomes errand boy and apprentice. His point of view, somewhere between those of Huckleberry Finn and Holden Caulfield, acts as a perfect foil to the violence he witnesses, occasionally neutralizing its effects but also giving the novel a sustained comic strain of a kind we have not seen in Doctorow before. A first reading suggests that *Billy Bathgate* is his best novel to date.

2

A Fiction for the Tribe: Toni Morrison's *The Bluest Eye*

by PETER DOUGHTY

> This civilisation of black people, which was underneath the white civilisation was there with its own everything. Everything of that civilisation was not worth hanging on to, but some of it was, and nothing has taken its place while it is being dismantled.[1]
>
> From my perspective there are only black people. When I say 'people' that's what I mean.[2]
>
> I write what I suppose could be called the tragic mode in which there is some catharsis and revelation. . . . Maybe it's a consequence of my being a classics minor.[3]

1

In a 1981 interview Thomas LeClair asked Toni Morrison, 'How do you conceive of your function as a writer?' She replied:

> I write what I have recently begun to call village literature, fiction that is really for the village, for the tribe. Peasant literature for *my* people. . . . I think long and carefully about what my novels ought to do. They should clarify the rôles that have become obscured; they ought to identify those things in the past that are useful and those that are not;

and they ought to give nourishment. . . . Now my people,
we 'peasants', have come to the city, that is to say we live
with its values. There is a confrontation between old values
of the tribe and new urban values. It's confusing. There has
to be a mode to do what music did for blacks, what we
used to be able to do in private and in that civilisation that
existed underneath the white civilisation. I think this accounts
for the address of my books. I am not explaining anything
to anybody. My work bears witness and suggests who the
outlaws were, who survived under what circumstances and
why, what was legal in the community as opposed to what
was legal outside it. All that is in the fabric of the story in
order to do what the music used to do. The music kept us
alive, but it's not enough any more. My people are being
devoured.[4]

The novel is seen as one of the means by which the
members of a cultural group come to share an understanding
of their experience: Morrison has said that writing fiction is
'a way to be coherent in the world'[5] and that as readers
'human beings organise their human knowledge'[6] through
the structures of narrative. In her attempt to sustain a
sense of cultural identity—what she means by 'nourishment'—for black Americans, her work may be seen as one
element in a much larger cultural undertaking. In critical
and polemical texts she has been approached in the context
of the development of a specifically committed group of
black women writers (though, as their careers have developed these writers have separated widely in their concerns):
Marjorie Pryse, for example, proposes that, 'In the 1970s and
1980s, black women novelists have become metaphorical
conjure women'[7] by re-establishing connections between
the contemporary reader and the nineteenth-century 'ancestors' in the black narrative tradition; and Barbara Christian
suggests that *The Bluest Eye* and Alice Walker's *The Third
Life of Grange Copeland*, both published in 1970, begin to
modify the address of black fiction, in that these novels
are written specifically for a black readership, explore the
interaction of race and gender in the experience of black
women, and offer a critical analysis of the internal relations
of 'the entire black community'.[8] In 1984 Michael G. Cooke
noted that a result of the activity of these and other black

writers in the '70s and '80s is an enhanced confidence in the centrality of black experience as literary material, resolving what had been a perpetual debate about the black writer's appropriate subject and audience: '. . . in the bearing of black literature today, "black experience" comes to the fore, without apology, without special pleading, without threat, without inhibition from without or within.'[9] Literary activity in turn should be seen in the context of a more general shift of attention during the late '60s and '70s from political to cultural relations between black and white America; a result of this shift is a radical reassessment of the traditional model of black American experience as at best dependent upon the wider culture, at worst as a 'pathological condition'[10] of it. A major project of black cultural nationalists, which black artists were called to promote, was to rewrite their own history: 'A rejection of the old history and standards demanded their replacement by a new history and standards which would redefine the meaning of black existence, past and present.'[11] Also during this period there was a considerable expansion of interest in black American culture among historians, sociologists, ethnographers, anthropologists, with a particular emphasis on the transmission and survival of African cultural practice and consciousness in the experience of black Americans.[12] The common concerns across this range of activity may be illustrated by putting Morrison's declaration in 1983 of her rôle as novelist for the tribe ('These people have a story, and that story has to be told. There was an articulate literature before there was print.'[13]) against Lawrence Levine's announcement of his intentions in *Black Culture and Black Consciousness* (1977):

> I have attempted to present and understand the thought of people who, though quite articulate in their own life-times, have been *rendered* historically inarticulate by scholars who have devoted their attention to other groups and other problems. . . .
>
> My efforts have led me to depart from the traditional historical practice of viewing the folk as inarticulate intellectual ciphers, as objects who were continually acted upon by forces over which they had no control, and to recognise them as

actors in their own right who not only responded to their situation but often affected it in crucial ways.[14]

What was happening in America, in turn, should be seen in the context of the work of cultural reclamation, with the novel as a critically important agent, being performed across the whole black diaspora. In 1964, the Nigerian novelist Chinua Achebe defined 'The Rôle of the Writer in a New Nation' in terms equally appropriate to the black writer in America:

> Historians everywhere are re-writing the stories of the new nations—replacing short, garbled, despised history with a more sympathetic account. . . . The worst thing that can happen to any people is the loss of their dignity and self-respect. The writer's duty is to help them regain it by showing them in human terms what happened to them, what they lost. . . . you need a writer to bring out the human tragedy, the crisis in the soul.[15]

In a 1965 essay, 'The Novelist as Teacher', he wrote:

> Here then is an adequate revolution for me to espouse—to help my society regain belief in itself and put away the complexes of the years of denigration and self-abasement. And it is essentially a question of education, in the best sense of that word.[16]

And in the West Indies, in the 1950s, as Gareth Griffiths explains:

> George Lamming sees the rise of the novel as providing for the first time 'a way of investigating and projecting the inner experience of the West Indian community'. For Lamming the resulting self-awareness is as important an event in West Indian history as the discovery of the islands, or the abolition of slavery and the influx of Asian labour in the nineteenth century. Even African writers have not seen their work as being so crucial, perhaps because for them the task was, in part, to recover and vitalise their own cultures. For the West Indian writer the task is to help create that distinctive culture.[17]

These declarations help to sense the scale of the project that Morrison is attempting in her novels: by producing a fiction for the tribe she is helping, in a radically important sense, to write the tribe into being. Taking her first novel *The Bluest Eye* (1970) as illustration, I want to explore the ways in which she is attempting to construct a history for her people, to identify threats to their culture and to personal identity, and to indicate the continuities and disruptions which make up that history.

2

To show what I think Morrison is doing with the cultural material accumulated in her first novel, I refer now to the narrative structures proposed by Robert Stepto in his richly provocative study, *From Behind the Veil* (1979), since these provide a useful way to explore the concerns and methods of *The Bluest Eye*, and allow us to relate the novel to other texts in the cultural tradition. Stepto traces the development of literary forms which articulate what he calls 'the primary pre-generic myth for Afro-America . . . the quest for freedom and literacy',[18] and which form the basis of a specifically Afro-American narrative tradition. He identifies 'two basic types of narrative expressions, the narratives of ascent and immersion'. Thus,

> The classic ascent narrative launches an 'enslaved' and semi-literate figure on a ritualised journey to a symbolic North; that journey is charted through spatial expressions of social structure, invariably systems of signs that the questing figure must read in order to be both increasingly literate and increasingly free. The ascent narrative conventionally ends with the questing figure situated in the least oppressive social structure afforded by the world of the narrative, and free in the sense that he or she has gained sufficient literacy to assume the mantle of an articulate survivor.

The immersion narrative inverts this structure: heading into a symbolic South, the questing figure ends up 'in or near the narrative's most oppressive social structure but free in the sense that he or she has gained sufficient tribal literacy to assume the mantle of articulate kinsman'.[19] Stepto feels that, after Wright's *Black Boy* (1937), 'the possibilities of significant revoicings' of these forms of narrative 'are virtually exhausted'. The logical next step is 'one that somehow creates a fresh narrative strategy and arc out of a remarkable combination of ascent and immersion narratives'; and he

33

sees the 'narrative of hibernation'[20] in *Invisible Man* (1952) as a
stage towards a new integration. This account seems to me to
suggest a helpful way of formulating what Morrison achieves
in *The Bluest Eye*: a way of describing the procedures of the
text is that she explores the relations between the two 'narrative expressions' through the experience of members of a
black neighbourhood in Lorain, Ohio, most of whom have
migrated from the South during the demographic transfor-
mations of the 1920s and 1930s, drawn north by 'the possibility of living better in another place'.[21] These characters enact
versions of the ascent narrative, in which the twin goals of
the myth, freedom and literacy, are ironically inflected. The
immersion narrative is implied by the structure of the text
itself; it is enacted, that is, within the consciousness of the
narrator.

The first of the novel's prologues signals that literacy is a
key issue: a paragraph from a 'Dick-and-Jane' first reading
primer, describing a white nuclear family happily occupying
a comfortable, green and white house, with pets and friends,
is printed conventionally, then with punctuation removed,
then with all spaces eliminated; progressively, as the structures of organization that give it meaning are removed, the
passage becomes unintelligible. Subsequently, each of the
novel's episodes is prefaced by an extract from this prologue,
ironically appropriate to the content of the episode: the story
of Cholly Breedlove's life of alienation, culminating in his
raping his daughter, is headed 'SEEFATHERHEISBIGAND-
STRONG' (122). Such a device has a number of elaborately
suggestive effects in relation to the narrative it introduces,
of which I would emphasize two: the stress on literacy as an
agency of cultural hegemony; and the ironic relation between
the icon and the actual experience of the black families
in the narrative, whose lives, in fact, form 'pathological'
versions of what the white primer suggests is the norm.[22]
The second prologue stresses the limits of freedom for Pecola
Breedlove, the young black girl whose tragedy is the novel's
principal narrative structure: her systematic victimization
and unnatural sexual experience (impregnated by her father,
the child dying), form an extreme version of the subjection
that all the characters experience in this novel. Each is

positioned specifically and definitively within the triangle of relations between literacy, sexuality and freedom.

The second prologue offers the novel as a particular kind of investigation into the circumstances of Pecola's life: '*since why is difficult to handle, one must take refuge in* how' (9). Pecola's experience is presented as a series of episodes in which she is victimized by members of her family and neighbourhood. Each episode is the culmination of an account of the personal experience of the victimizer, which in turn is designed to explain in historical terms why he/she treats Pecola in this way. In each episode the psychic damage sustained by Pecola becomes more extensive. After some encounters with children, who use her as the adults also do, to confirm their own identity and status, Pecola encounters Geraldine; the narrative now probes backwards into Geraldine's personal history, and presents her as representative of a particular kind of black experience—following one contour of the ascent narrative. Geraldine is characterized as one of the 'sugar-brown' girls from Mobile, Aiken, Newport News, Meridian—from middle-class 'quiet black neighbourhoods where everybody is gainfully employed' (76), and life is organized around the twin principles of assimilation to white culture and exclusion of everything black; in this contour, achieving literacy is learning to serve the white man:

> They go to land-grant colleges, normal schools, and learn how to do the white man's work with refinement: home economics to prepare his food; teacher education to instruct black children in obedience; music to soothe the weary master and entertain his blunted soul. Here they learn the rest of the lesson begun in those soft houses with porch swings and pots of bleeding heart: how to behave. The careful development of thrift, patience, high morals, and good manners. In short, how to get rid of the funkiness. The dreadful funkiness of passion, the funkiness of nature, the funkiness of the wide range of human emotions. (77)

Finding Pecola in her home, Geraldine sees in her all the disorder she fears for herself and her family; Pecola is what she is escaping from:

> The girls grew up knowing nothing of girdles, and the boys

35

announced their manhood by turning the bills of their caps
backward. Grass wouldn't grow where they lived. Flowers
died. Shades fell down. Tin cans and tires blossomed where
they lived. They lived on cold black-eyed beans and orange
pop. Like flies they hovered; like flies they settled. And this
one had settled in her house. Up over the hump of the cat's
back she looked.

'Get out,' she said, her voice very quiet. 'You nasty little
black bitch. Get out of my house.' (86)

As Susan Willis says, in Morrison's work 'sexuality con-
verges with history, and functions as a register for the experience of change, i.e., historical transition.'[23] Geraldine's
fastidiousness, her commitment to order and control, her
alienation from the passion and energy she associates with
the idea of blackness, register in her inability to love
(she looks after her son's needs but gives her affection
to her cat) and, in particular, her incapacity for sexual
pleasure:

> [Her husband] must enter her surreptitiously, lifting the hem
> of her nightgown only to her navel. . . . She hopes he will
> not sweat—the damp may get into her hair; and that she will
> remain dry between her legs—she hates the glucking sound
> they make when she is moist. (79)

In the case of Pecola's mother, Pauline, the analysis
is more extended, but the narrative procedure is similar. Young and recently married, brought north in the
1920s from Alabama to an alien community with unfamiliar
practices and more white people in regular contact than she
has been accustomed to, she finds compensation for her
loneliness and sense of her own ugliness in the movies,
where she learns to read a system of signs that constitute
herself and her family as negligible. This form of cultural
literacy imprisons her consciousness: 'In equating physical
beauty with virtue, she stripped her mind, bound it, and
collected self-contempt by the heap' (113). Entering service
with a white family, 'she became what is known as an ideal
servant, for such a rôle filled practically all of her needs'
(117). In the white home 'she could arrange things, clean
things, line things up in neat rows', and indulge a passion

for the order and beauty that her own home life, in the South as well as the North, has systematically denied her. As Willis says, she 'lives a form of schizophrenia'[24] which foreshadows her daughter's breakdown at the end of the novel:

> Pauline kept this order, this beauty, for herself, a private world, and never introduced it into her storefront, or to her children. Them she bent toward respectability, and in so doing taught them fear: fear of being clumsy, fear of being like their father, fear of not being loved by God, fear of madness like Cholly's mother. Into her son she beat a loud desire to run away, and into her daughter she beat a fear of growing up, fear of other people, fear of life. (119)

When her daughter intrudes into the white home and frightens the 'little pink-and-yellow girl', Pauline punishes Pecola and comforts the white child; later, she beats her pregnant daughter into a premature delivery. Again personal and cultural dislocation is registered sexually; unlike the bourgeois Geraldine, Pauline has a peasant's memory of the sexual pleasure that is now beyond her, replaced by religious respectability:

> *I begin to feel those little bits of color floating up into me—deep in me. That streak of green from the june-bug light, the purple from the berries trickling along my thighs, Mama's lemonade yellow runs sweet in me. Then I feel like I'm laughing between my legs, and the laughing gets all mixed up with the colors, and I'm afraid I'll come, and afraid I won't. But I know I will. And I do. And it be rainbow all inside. . . .*
> *But it ain't like that anymore. Most times he's thrashing away inside me before I'm woke, and through when I am. The rest of the time I can't even be next to his stinking drunk self. But I don't care 'bout it no more. My Maker will take care of me. I know He will. I know He will.* (121)

Cholly Breedlove, abandoned by his father and mother, brought up by his Great Aunt Jimmy in a rural black community in Georgia, is, when she dies, brutally rejected a second time by his father, and becomes 'dangerously free', though he never achieves literacy:

37

Abandoned in a junk heap by his mother, rejected for a
crap game by his father, there was nothing more to lose. He
was alone with his perceptions and appetites, and they alone
interested him. (147)

The wandering Cholly meets and marries Pauline Williams
in Tennessee and with her heads north to the steel mills of
Ohio, to occupy a dilapidated storefront apartment where—
in the depression years—the marriage collapses into alternating rituals of violence and sex. Reeling home drunk one
Saturday afternoon, aroused to sympathy and passion when
his daughter unconsciously repeats a gesture her mother
had made when Cholly first saw her, he rapes Pecola, who
conceives; the baby is born prematurely and dies; Pecola
goes mad.

Morrison says she is particularly interested in, and sympathetic towards, these characters 'in motion', of whom Cholly
is the first instance in her work, and whose existential condition of freedom—what she calls 'wildness', in her interview
with Claudia Tate—'has bad effects in society such as the
one in which we live.'[25] 'In the process of finding,' she says
in another interview, 'they are also making themselves.'[26]
Cholly, Ajax (*Sula*), Guitar (*Song of Solomon*), and Son Green
(*Tar Baby*), having been in a sense formed by their history,
nevertheless *choose* their track through the world: 'They
express either an effort of the will or a freedom of the will.
It's all about choosing. Though granted there's an enormous
amount of stuff one cannot choose.' They are, that is, like black
Americans at large, both victims and agents in their own history: 'They are the misunderstood people in the world.'[27] In
the novel, the narrator perceives that the rape was ironically
an act of love: 'He, at any rate, was the one who loved her
enough to touch her, envelop her, give her something of himself. But his touch was fatal . . .' (189).

For what is to be the final stage of her demoralization,
Pecola goes to ask Soaphead Church, the neighbourhood's
priest/medicine-man, 'Reader, Adviser, and Interpreter of
Dreams', for her eyes to be turned blue (as she has prayed for
a year to have them become). Soaphead, following another
contour of the ascent narrative, is a 'cinnamon-eyed West
Indian with lightly browned skin', descendant of a family

'proud of its accomplishments and its mixed blood—in fact they believed the former was based on the latter', whose ancestors separated themselves 'in body, mind and spirit from all that suggested Africa', and who arrives in Lorain in 1936. His special kind of literacy (a wide but selective reading in European literature, though allowing 'only the narrowest interpretation to touch him' (156)) gives him the freedom of misanthropy (151), a licence to exploit and manipulate the black community he despises. Morrison said about him:

> . . . he would be wholly convinced that if black people were more like white people they would be better off. And I tried to explain that in terms of his own West Indian background—a kind of English, colonial, Victorian thing drilled into his head which he could not escape. I needed someone to distill all of that, to say, 'Yeah, you're right, you need them. Here, I'll give them to you,' and really believe that he had done her a favour. . . . That kind of black.[28]

Doing her a favour, Soaphead also uses her to poison a dog whose messy senility offends him ('If the animal behaves strangely, your wish will be granted on the day following this one' (162)). Believing her wish granted, Pecola declines into madness, finally achieving a voice in the dialogue between the two parts of her consciousness, endlessly debating the beauty of the colour of her eyes. Soaphead, who 'could have been an active homosexual but lacked the courage' (153), whose marriage was wrecked by his equating 'lovemaking with communion and the Holy Grail' (157), likes to play with young girls; his paedophilia forms what Barbara Christian calls a 'thematic chord'[29] with Mr. Henry's molesting Frieda (for which he is run off by her father with a gun) and Cholly's rape of his own daughter.

The effects of these various kinds of mutilation, ironically 'in the least oppressive structure afforded by the world of the narrative', are concentrated into the final image of Pecola:

> The damage done was total. She spent her days, her tendril, sap-green days, walking up and down, her head jerking to

the beat of a drummer so distant only she could hear. Elbows bent, hands on shoulders, she flailed her arms like a bird in an eternal, grotesquely futile effort to fly. Beating the air, a winged but grounded bird, intent on the blue void it could not reach—could not even see—but which filled the valleys of the mind. (188)

What Barbara Smith calls the 'manifold and simultaneous oppressions that all women of colour face . . . the demoralization of being female *and* coloured *and* poor *and* hated'[30] are compounded in Pecola's experience by her youth and her ugliness. The extreme but exemplary nature of her subjection is indicated by Morrison's use here of the motif of flight, which is important throughout her work as signifying transcendence that leads to freedom and self-knowledge (both denied Pecola). For the structure of *Song of Solomon* (1977) she draws on the legend that Africans could fly but lost the ability when they were brought to America and ate salt; slaves who recovered the power escaped bondage by flying back to Africa.[31] In *Sula* (1973) Ajax's love of aeroplanes, his longing to fly the machine whose use is exclusive to white men, relates him ironically to the legend: he escapes not to Africa but to the air show in Dayton.[32] Pecola's aspiration to flight—as fruitless as her longing for death, invisibility and blue eyes (43–5)—is another ironic reminder of the actual condition of her life in the Northern community.

The Northern experience is counterpointed by the representation of Southern black culture. Aunt Jimmy's rescue of Cholly, the support she gets from the community during her terminal illness, and the communal ritual of her funeral contrast with the insulated nuclearity of families in the North, where only the McTeers support Pecola, when her father sets fire to the storefront. In Georgia, the boundaries between household and community virtually disappear when Aunt Jimmy is taken ill. M'Dear, called in to attend, is the first of Morrison's conjure women, whose power, like that of Circe in *Song of Solomon*, is registered sexually: as Cholly falls asleep listening to the women talk, 'In a dream his penis changed into a long hickory stick, and the hands caressing it were the hands of M'Dear' (129). This episode contains Morrison's most sustained and unequivocal—but also elegiac—celebration of the resilience and integrity of black women:

> But they had been young once. The odor of their armpits and haunches had mingled into a lovely musk; their eyes had been furtive, their lips relaxed, and the delicate turn of their heads on those slim black necks had been nothing other than a doe's. Their laughter had been more touch than sound.
> Then they had grown. Edging into life from the back door. Becoming. Everybody in the world was in a position to give them orders. White women said, 'Do this.' White children said, 'Give me that.' White men said, 'Come here.' Black men said, 'Lay down.' The only people they need not take orders from were black children and each other. But they took all of that and recreated it in their own image. They ran the houses of white people and knew it. When white men beat their men, they cleaned up the blood and went home to receive abuse from the victim. They beat their children with one hand and stole for them with the other. The hands that felled trees also cut umbilical cords; the hands that wrung the necks of chickens and butchered hogs also nudged African violets into bloom; the arms that loaded sheaves, bales, and sacks rocked babies into sleep. They patted biscuits into flaky ovals of innocence—and shrouded the dead. They plowed all day and came home to nestle like plums under the limbs of their men. The legs that straddled a mule's back were the same ones that straddled their men's hips. And the difference was all the difference there was.
> Then they were old. Their bodies honed, their odor sour. Squatting in a cane field, stooping in a cotton field, kneeling by a river bank, they had carried a world in their heads. They had given over the lives of their own children and tendered their grandchildren. (127–28)

This is a powerful endorsement and reminder of 'the old values of the tribe', whose absence in the Northern neighbourhood makes Pecola's tragedy possible. The irony that these values were generated in 'the narrative's most oppressive social structure' is registered in the trauma experienced by Cholly when his sexual initiation is disturbed by white hunters, who force him to continue while they watch and jeer (136): his rite of passage interrupted, but fearing to hate the white men, he turns his hatred on the girl, on his own kind; the association of brutality as well as tenderness with sexuality marks his later relations with Pauline and Pecola.

In her exploration of black cultural history ('the weight of history working its way out in the life of one, two, three people . . . a large idea, brought down small and at home'[33]) Morrison tests the range of ironies secreted within the narratives that Stepto describes, and brings together the rôles of articulate survivor and articulate kinswoman in the consciousness of the narrator. Claudia McTeer's maturing vision is suggested by an extremely simple device. The novel is organized into four sequences, each associated with a season, beginning with Autumn 1940; each of these sequences begins with a reflection from Claudia on her memories of that season, in which, as Phyllis Klotman notes, the right-hand margin is free form, 'like the handwriting of a child'.[34] Each of these meditations is followed by one or more episodes of Pecola's victimization, with explanatory history of the victimizer, in which the text is right justified, presumably to indicate a more mature consciousness—perhaps a different, impersonal, narrator. However, in the last section of the novel, where, undoubtedly, we hear Claudia's voice, the margin is also right justified, perhaps indicating Claudia's own eventual capacity for more organized reflection. At the end of the novel, therefore, we realize that the personal histories are recounted not by a different narrator in the same time sequence, but by the same narrator at a different time: with Claudia, as we read forward in Pecola's narrative, we are also reading backward in the personal histories of the other characters, to discover not only the how—but also the why—explanation of the novel's events; this is also to read back from the North in the present of the event into an immersion in the South and the past: as Morrison said, about the structures of both *The Bluest Eye* and *Sula*, 'if you go back to the beginnings, you get pushed along towards the end. This is particularly so with *The Bluest Eye*.'[35] The conclusion for Claudia, Morrison says, is the same as for Milkman Dead, Jadine, and Nel: 'They learn something . . . there is a press towards knowledge, at the expense of happiness, perhaps.'[36] What Claudia learns from the events in the North derives from a number of sources: her own observation; personal testimony (Pauline's section is in part in first-person reminiscence); her understanding of the community in the South and the history that connects it to the North; and the security of her own family, which enables her to recognize the importance of its absence in Pecola's life. This last factor is crucial, since the family embodies the central values that the novel proposes. The beginning of the Winter section positions Mr. McTeer tellingly as a pioneer ('Wolf killer turned hawk fighter, he worked night and day to keep one from the door and the other from under the windowsills' (59)), protecting his family from, but also bringing civilization to, the Northern frontier. Retaining, in the North, aspects of Southern community, Claudia's family is evoked with a quality of delight that attaches to no other family in Morrison's work:

> But was it really like that? As painful as I remember? Only mildly. Or rather it was a productive and fructifying pain. Love, thick and dark as Alaga syrup, eased up into that cracked window. I could smell it—taste it—sweet, musty, with an edge of wintergreen in its base—everywhere in that house. It stuck, along with my tongue, to the frosted window-panes. It coated my chest, along with the salve, and when the flannel came undone in my sleep, the clear, sharp curves of air outlined its presence on my throat. And in the night, when my coughing was dry and tough, feet padded into the room, hands repinned the flannel, readjusted the quilt, and rested a moment on my forehead. So when I think of autumn, I think of somebody with hands who does not want me to die. (15)

Claudia's version of the ascent narrative is the process of coming to understand the 'revelation' of Pecola's tragedy and her community's rôle in it: that is, she learns the conditions of the North and writes as articulate survivor. Perceiving the continuity of black experience she writes as articulate kinswoman. Literate in both the dominant cultural system of signs (she perceives the real meaning of the Shirley Temple doll) and the tribal system (initiated by sympathetic kinship), she can read the meaning of Pecola's experience, in which she is herself involved:

All of our waste which we dumped on her and which she absorbed. And all of our beauty which was hers first, and which she gave to us. All of us—all who knew her—felt so wholesome after we cleaned ourselves on her. We were so beautiful when we stood astride her ugliness. (189)

Barbara Christian suggests that Pecola's desire for blue eyes, the white model of beauty, 'encompasses three hundred years of unsuccessful interface between black and white culture'[37]; but the novel also insists that, as Cynthia Davis says, 'blacks have choice within the context of oppression.'[38] The culture colludes in its own mutilation by attaching both approval and opprobrium to the wrong things: mothers give their children Shirley Temple dolls ('I knew that the doll represented what they thought was my fondest wish' (22)) and blame them for the flaws of the adult world (' "She carry some of the blame. . . . How come she didn't fight him?" ' (175)) At this level of meaning Pecola, scapegoat and pariah for her own community, also embodies the relation of black culture to white. Morrison says,

the concept of the black in this country is almost always one of the pariah. But a community contains pariahs within it that are very useful for the conscience of the community.[39]

The community's 'use' of its pariahs, however, reveals its own moral condition; just as Pecola's value to her neighbours is to confirm their beauty by her ugliness, the service that blacks do whites is to confirm their sense of superiority.

As I have suggested, Claudia eventually perceives the cycle of events as tragic, but it is a tragedy shaped by the circumstances of a specific history. In her final meditation Claudia refuses the option to read her story as fatally determined; there is responsibility to allocate:

This soil is bad for certain kinds of flowers. Certain seeds it will not nurture, certain fruit it will not bear, and when the land kills of its own volition, we acquiesce and say the victim had no right to live. We are wrong, of course, but it doesn't matter. It's too late. At least on the edge of my town, among the garbage and the sunflowers of my town, it's much, much, much too late. (190)

The repetition of 'my town' intimates the beginning of a new, responsible sense of Northern community, with the idea of the family at its heart, written into being by the understanding of black American experience that Claudia has constructed from the events of the year covered by the novel. The nature of this new awareness is indicated ironically by Claudia's echo of the penultimate paragraph of Richard Wright's *Black Boy*, where the protagonist is preparing to leave for the North:

> Yet, deep down, I knew that I could never leave the South, for my feelings had already been formed by the South, for there had been slowly instilled into my personality and consciousness, black though I was, the culture of the South. So, in leaving, I was taking a part of the South to transplant in alien soil, to see if it could grow differently, if it could drink of new and cool rains, bend in strange winds, respond to the warmth of other suns, and, perhaps, to bloom. . . . And if that miracle ever happened, then I would know that there was yet hope in that southern swamp of despair and violence, that light could emerge even out of the blackest of the southern night.[40]

Wright is writing himself into an ascent narrative where literacy is liberation from what he sees as 'the cultural barrenness of black life':

> After I had outlived the shocks of childhood, after the habit of reflection had been born in me, I used to mull over the strange absence of real kindness in Negroes, how unstable was our tenderness, how lacking in genuine passion we were, how void of great hope, how timid our joy, how bare our traditions, how hollow our memories, how lacking we were in those intangible sentiments that bind man to man, and how shallow was even our despair.[41]

Stepto suggests that this and other 'controversial' passages from *Black Boy* call into being vigorous responses from later generations of black American writers, including Morrison.[42] The echo between the texts reinforces Morrison's profound repudiation of this view of black culture. Where Wright suggests that individual hope lies in recovery from 'that southern swamp of despair and violence' through contact with a wider society, Morrison insists that the culture generated in the South contained elements of value that the wider society is destroying. Wright's perception of the cultural

45

barrenness of black experience in the South, of course, has
been generally shared. Ralph Ellison, for example, writes in
'Richard Wright's Blues', that the 'distinctive character'
of Southern Negro culture, rather than being a positively
supportive structure, was 'very much in the nature of an
elaborate but limited defense mechanism',[43] and he also,
in this essay at least, perceives the Northern migration
unequivocally as culturally liberating:

> Intelligence tests have measured the quick rise in intellect
> which takes place in Southern Negroes after moving North,
> but little attention has been paid to the mutations effected in
> their sensibilities. However, the two go hand in hand. Intel-
> lectual complexity is accompanied by emotional complexity;
> refinement of thought by refinement of feeling. The movement
> north affects more than the Negro's wage scale, it affects his
> entire psychosomatic structure.[44]

Morrison complicates this model of black experience dramatically, since in her novel, characteristically, the enhanced sensibility achieved by Claudia is associated with a view of black
history as tragic in quite a different way from that proposed
by Ellison: where he perceives black culture as smothering
individual identity, Morrison sees its erosion as exposing
the individual to chaos, or another kind of thraldom. Where
Tony Tanner identifies the predominant preoccupation of the
texts he considers in *City of Words* as 'an abiding dream . . .
that an unpatterned, unconditioned life is possible, in which
your movements and stillnesses, choices and repudiations are
all your own',[45] Morrison, like other black writers, dreams
of a tribe, a village—where individuality did not mean
isolation, but rather where 'there were spaces and places
in which a single person could enter and behave as an
individual within the context of the community.'[46]

3

One of my purposes in invoking Stepto's models is to suggest that an important element of Morrison's achievement in
her first novel is that she presents to her readers a version
of their own historical experience which is derived from the
resources and narrative traditions of their own culture; and

in each of her subsequent novels she inflects in different ways the narrative forms I have been considering. However, the effect of the structure, characterization, and organization of time in *The Bluest Eye* is to stress historical determinism as explanation: it is not only Pecola who may be seen, as Morrison says, as 'a total and complete victim of whatever was around her',[47] since all the characters are constructed by narratives designed to 'explain' how they come to be what they are. This organization of material, characteristic of naturalism, severely limits the writer's ability to present her characters, and the black community that they represent, as 'actors in their own right', in Levine's words. One of the problems that her subsequent novels tackle in different ways, therefore, is to enlarge the scope of choice, and therefore both personal and communal responsibility, for her characters—to increase the scale of their 'relative autonomy', to grant them agency in their own history. In *Sula* (1973) she does this by bracketing off the history of the Bottom from direct white intervention between the 1860s and the 1960s, and by making each of her central characters realize an independent self: Shadrack through madness and his discovery of his blackness; Nel by an ironic immersion narrative which takes her to New Orleans but brings her back thinking ' "I'm me. I'm not their daughter. . . . I'm me. Me" '[48]; and Sula by an ironic ascent narrative which takes her around the United States and back to live and die in Medallion, having chosen her solitude (' ". . . my lonely is *mine* . . . your lonely is someone else's" '[49]). Milkman Dead in *Song of Solomon* (1977) follows a complete contour of the immersion narrative from his northern city to discover his identity and genealogy in the deep South: as Cynthia Davis points out in her helpful essay, Morrison preserves the valency of the myths she invokes in this novel, not only by excluding white people almost entirely,[50] but also by 'correcting' the myths to reflect 'a new definition of heroism'. In *Tar Baby* (1981) Morrison 'revoices' the two narrative forms spectacularly to emphasize both the personal imperatives of her characters and a deeply pessimistic view of the fatal erosion of black American culture: Son and Jadine test the ascent narrative by their sojourn in New York and the immersion narrative by their visit to Eloe, Florida; when these ventures fail, each character completes a narrative logic by leaving the United States altogether, Jadine for Paris and Son for the hinterland of the Caribbean island to join the blind horsemen in the hills. In *Beloved* (1987) Morrison constructs a full version of the ascent narrative, with an insistence on individual will, an extraordinarily complex time structure, a powerfully tragic charge, and her fullest exploration of the 'great supernatural element'[51] of black consciousness. This novel, I suspect, will be a major turning-point in her writing.

NOTES

1. Toni Morrison, interview in *The Soho News*, 11 March 1981, p. 2.
2. Thomas LeClair, 'The Language Must Not Sweat: A Conversation with Toni Morrison', *New Republic*, 21 March 1981, p. 28.
3. Ibid., p. 28.
4. Ibid., p. 26.
5. Ibid., p. 22.
6. Jane S. Bakerman, 'The Seams Can't Show: An Interview with Toni Morrison', *Black American Literature Forum*, 12, No. 2 (1978), 58.
7. In Marjorie Pryse and Hortense J. Spillers (eds.), *Conjuring: Black Women, Fiction and Literary Tradition* (Bloomington: Indiana University Press, 1985), p. 5.
8. Ibid., p. 240.
9. Michael G. Cooke, *Afro-American Literature in the Twentieth Century: The Achievement of Intimacy* (New Haven: Yale University Press, 1984), p. 210.
10. The formulation is Gunnar Myrdal's: *An American Dilemma* (New York: Harper & Row, 1962), p. 929.
11. Frances and Val Gray Ward, 'The Black Artist: His Rôle in the Struggle', *The Black Scholar*, 2, No. 5 (January 1971), p. 27. See also Harry Reed, 'Toni Morrison, *Song of Solomon* and Black Cultural Nationalism', *Centennial Review*, 32, No. 1 (1987), 50–64.
12. See Melville J. Herskovits, *The Myth of the Negro Past* (Gloucester, Mass.: Peter Smith, 1970) for an early survey of this issue (1941).
13. Nellie McKay, interview with Toni Morrison, *Contemporary Literature*, 24, No. 4 (Winter, 1983), 427.
14. Lawrence Levine, *Black Culture and Black Consciousness* (New York: Oxford University Press, 1977), pp. ix–xi.

15. G. D. Killam (ed.), *African Writers on African Writing* (London: Heinemann, 1973), pp. 7–13.
16. Ibid., p. 3; see also Evelyn Hawthorne, 'On Gaining the Double Vision; *Tar Baby* as Diasporean Novel', *Black American Literature Forum*, 2, No. 1 (1988), 97–107, and Vashti Crutcher Lewis, 'African Tradition in Toni Morrison's *Sula*', *Phylon*, 48, No. 1 (1987), 91–7.
17. Gareth Griffiths, *A Double Exile: African and West Indian Writing Between Two Cultures* (London: Marion Boyars, 1978), p. 91.
18. Robert B. Stepto, *From Behind the Veil* (Urbana: University of Illinois, 1979), p. ix.
19. Ibid., p. 167.
20. Ibid., p. 193.
21. Toni Morrison, *The Bluest Eye* (London: Triad, Grafton Books, 1988), p. 103; all subsequent references are given in parentheses in the text.
22. The effect is to contradict Myrdal, who argued that 'it is to the advantage of American Negroes as individuals and as a group to become assimilated to American culture . . .'; Morrison suggests that the attempt to assimilate is what causes the pathology.
23. Susan Willis, 'Eruptions of Funk: Historicising Toni Morrison', *Black American Literature Forum*, 16, No. 1 (1982), 34.
24. Ibid., p. 35.
25. Claudia Tate (ed.), interview with Toni Morrison in *Black Women Writers at Work* (New York: Continuum, 1983), p. 126.
26. Robert Stepto, 'Intimate Things in Place': interview with Toni Morrison, *Massachusetts Review*, 18, No. 3 (1977), p. 486.
27. Tate, p. 126.
28. Stepto interview, p. 483.
29. Barbara Christian, *Black Women Novelists: The Development of a Tradition* (Westport, Conn.: Greenwood Press, 1980), p. 145.
30. Barbara Smith, *Home Girls: A Black Feminist Anthology* (New York: Kitchen Table: Women of Color Press, 1983), pp. xxxii–xxxiv.
31. Dorothy H. Lee, '*Song of Solomon*: To Ride the Air', *Black American Literature*, 16, No. 2 (1982), 64–70.
32. Toni Morrison, *Sula* (London: Triad, Grafton Books, 1988), pp. 114–20.
33. Stepto interview, p. 489.
34. Phyllis R. Klotman, 'Dick-and-Jane and the Shirley Temple Sensibility in *The Bluest Eye*', *Black American Literature Forum*, 13, No. 4 (1979), 123.
35. Tate, p. 124.
36. McKay, interview with Toni Morrison, p. 424.
37. Christian, *Black Women Novelists*, p. 138.
38. Cynthia A. Davis, 'Self, Society and Myth in Toni Morrison's Fiction', *Contemporary Literature*, 23, No. 3 (Summer, 1982) 335.
39. Tate, p. 129.
40. Richard Wright, *Black Boy* (New York: Harper & Row, 1966), p. 284.
41. Ibid., p. 45.

42. Stepto, *From Behind the Veil*, p. 160.
43. Ralph Ellison, *Shadow and Act* (New York: Vintage, 1972), p. 90.
44. Ibid., p. 88.
45. Tony Tanner, *City of Words* (London: Jonathan Cape, 1971), p. 15.
46. Toni Morrison in Mari Evans (ed.), *Black Women Writers* (London: Pluto Press, 1985), p. 339.
47. Stepto interview, p. 479.
48. Toni Morrison, *Sula*, p. 32.
49. Ibid., p. 127.
50. Davis, p. 335.
51. McKay, interview with Toni Morrison, p. 428; see also G. Michelle Collins, 'There Where We Are Not: The Magical Real in *Beloved* and *Mama Day*', *Southern Review—Baton*, 24, No. 3 (1988), 680–85.

3

The Real Needs of Man: Don DeLillo's Novels

by ERIC MOTTRAM

DeLillo's work organizes the coherence and obsession with coherence that marks a novelist who needs closed plot as the example of a certain human need: for the total, for deep, inclusive system, network, organization, enclosure with rules and rituals, secrecy, conspiracy—the structures of power, or, in a phrase from *Running Dog*, 'the narrowing of choices'. Monadic system has long been a human obsession, but DeLillo's novels are part of a late twentieth-century fascination with covert behaviour—spies and counter spies, M.I.5, the rigmarole exposed for its cruel futility in John Huston's *The Kremlin Letter* (1970), the market for spy books and films, the ubiquitous C.I.A., the information and security rackets, surveillance mania, insane ideological alibis, and so on. The global village is presented as (and in fact is) an interlocked irrational system of the kind once reserved for religions but now a rabid quasi-secular design. Sacrifice to principle or the need to dominate is repeatedly written up as erotic success story for those whose power for pleasure is its own nutrition. Bataille's patterns of sacrificial desire are barely concealed as world-government: a 'radial matrix', a key term in *Running Dog*, DeLillo's sardonic 1978 farce of erotic conspiracy.[1] Manic terrorism endlessly emerges from processes of permissive innocence—permission, that is, to act freely out of the cover of any system whose desire is fulfilment through control, operating towards ultimate controls of captivity, enslavement and death. DeLillo works where utopia and dystopia are indistinguishable; his plots confer enjoyable reading on their systems, but also infer our conspiracy to enter their networks. The theory of paranoia does not enter his fictions; unlike Thomas Pynchon, he dramatizes the conditions of vigorous action and pleasure within network without narrowing the psycho-philosophical options into a solutionary programme. In fact, catastrophe is not so much a climax as a continuous eventuality, the processes of a world of perpetual emergency. The C.I.A., a main component of *Libra* in 1988, is frequently mentioned in earlier texts as a prime example of the perpetuation of warfare as unceasing covert assault, a system for which peace is an irritating anomaly. But obsession with interacting paths of behaviour to form a network of connections—the plot basis of *Our Mutual Friend*, *Daniel Deronda* and *Tess of the D'Urbervilles*—reaches beyond the local and national. DeLillo's understanding of language and numerology, and their relations with technology and erotics, is in a class apart.

He begins with the knowledge that privacy has shrunk to an exceptional condition; that late twentieth-century existence is exceptionally public and designed; that choice is increasingly an illusion, even increasingly disliked and feared: 'Choice is a subtle form of disease' (*Running Dog*, III, 3). Just as a C.I.A. character, obsessed with plot and death as bases of fatality and need, expresses it in *Libra*—so, in an interview, DeLillo is explicit that it is the basis for *White Noise*:

> Plots carry their own logic. There is a tendency of plots to move toward death. He believed that the idea of death is woven into the nature of every plot. A narrative plot is no less than a conspiracy of armed men. . . . A plot in fiction, he believed, is the way we localize the force of the death outside the book, play it off, contain it. The ancients staged mock battles to parallel the tempests in nature and reduce their fear of gods who warred in the sky.

Plot is therefore the extension of a real need to reveal that, 'there is a world inside the world', and precisely here generates manic obsession with investigation and assemblage of research: there must be meaning somewhere, even if invented, the crazed impulses of ideologists and the religious.

Since it is unlikely that DeLillo's novels will be familiar to most readers, this essay will assess each of the texts in order to consider, briefly, how each develops a series of related themes which, while given different locations, achieve a coherence and development related to what I refer in my title as the 'real' needs of man.

Americana (1971) exposes American television's parasitic use of people's lives, a virus needing a host. Kafka's 'The Great Wall of China' becomes, in Chapter 4, a critique and endorsement, a paradigm of future DeLillo considerations of the social and its hidden designs. At a pre-Christmas T.V. network conference, an executive asserts: 'At this juncture . . . the World War III idea is about forty per cent less viable than it was a week ago.' 'Indians' are also clichés to be refurbished—'Richter actually knows an Indian. Old fraternity brother.' Mao's Long March, the 'China thing', could be a series basis, but a 'viewpoint' has to be worked out with the State Department. The network's head then cites Kafka's story as a viable point of view:

> Every fellow-countryman was a brother for whom one was building a wall of protection, and who would return lifelong thanks for it with all he had and did. Unity! Unity! Shoulder to shoulder, a ring of brothers, a current of blood no longer confined within the narrow circulation of one body, but sweetly rolling throughout the endless leagues of China.

'It encapsulates all the surging drama of a land mass whose people we can only guess at. Where did you get that tie?'—'It really sings, Ted. May be your girl can type it up for me.' So the closed organization recognizes its own; one of Kafka's many anxious exposures of totalitarian invention is read as straight endorsement. In Erich Heller's words: 'Kafka's hero is the man who *believes* in absolute freedom, but cannot have any conception of it because he *exists* in a world of slavery.'[2] David Bell, the first-person narrator of the novel and T.V. producer, listens to Mingus, Ornette

Coleman, Bartok, cowboy songs, and so forth, on his car radio, as ego necessities. Like his associates and the masses they control, he lives a fiction extended from T.V., film, commercials and anything he cares to summon up as 'media'. His narrative is 'my very own commercial, a life within a life', plotted as a fiction for a production system. DeLillo's massive detail presents a lively, infatuated monster at the centre of American need. Gaps between self and society as network are closed by the involutions of productivity, propaganda, and the reasons of State:

> For propaganda to *succeed*, it must correspond to a need for propaganda on the individual's part. . . . The propagandee is by no means just an innocent victim. He provokes the psychological action of propaganda, and not merely lends himself to it, but even desires satisfaction from it. . . . Propaganda is needed in the exercise of power for the simple reason that the masses have come to participate in political affairs. Let us not call this democracy . . . the mass knows its rules through the press, radio and TV. . . .

The media operate as semi-secret behaviour controls whose effects constitute bases for further policies of control, within the efficiencies of technological society: 'True modern propaganda can only function within the context of the modern scientific system.' T.V. is peculiarly suited:

> Modern man deeply craves friendship, confidence, close personal relationships. But he is plunged into a world of competition, hostility and anonymity. . . . TV creates feelings of friendship, a new intimacy. . . . purely illusory and fallacious because there is no true friendship of any kind between the TV personality and the viewer who feels that personality to be his friend. . . . TV reaches him at home, like radio, in his own setting, his private life . . . but has the shock effect of the picture, which is much greater than that of sound.[3]

DeLillo's network uses Fellini and Bergman films to create part of its style-image. T.V. rôles are played as directed by the film-controller. *Americana* presents acting, actors and action as performances out of propaganda decisions, and the network employees know this. Meta-theatre, in Lionel

Abel's well-known sense, has become meta-society and its meta-fictions.[4]

But Bell narrates from a Mediterranean coast facing Africa, rehearsing a life of such fictional systematization. He recalls how drug language and media language interchanged:

> The war was on television every night but we all went to the movies. Soon most movies began to look alike and we went into dim rooms and turned on or off, or watched others turn on or off, of burned joss sticks and listened to tapes in near silence. Then we invented anti-orgies. (These were touchless events by and large, perhaps inspired, ultimately, by film clips of the interrupted war—full circle for technetronic man.)

The network simulates all organizational life in DeLillo:

> Hidden energies filled their air, small currents, as happens in every business which thrives in the heat of the image. There was a cult of the unattractive and the clever. There were points scored for ruthlessness.

The memos he receives from someone called Trotsky—on Zwingli, Rilke, Lévi-Strauss, Chekhov, Tillich, Blake, Charles Olson and 'a Kiowa chief named Satanta'—all feed into the system: 'We seemed to be no more than electronic signals and we moved through time and space with the stutter and shadowed insanity of a T.V. commercial.' Like Burroughs, Bell takes the past to be film reels: 'There are no old times . . . the tapes have been accidentally destroyed.' He courts his wife Meredith on 'Americana' literary and film images, and it destroys them. He becomes a figure that culminates in the C.I.A. hoodlums of *Libra* seventeen years later—in fact, the following passage reads now like a resumé of *Libra's* plot:

> I began to understand the attraction of pathological lying. To construct one's own reality, then bend it into an implausible extreme . . . an adventure even more thrilling than the linguistic free falls of the network. . . . my whole life was a lesson in the effect of echoes . . . I was lying in the third person.

Driving across America, he exemplifies media-addiction, within exactly the car image McLuhan proposed in his studies of media in 1965:

I was wearing green military-advisor sunglasses, a pair of wolf-hide moccasins, black chinos, a tight T-shirt and khaki cap cocked low over my eyes. . . . The windows were closed and the heater on and I moaned and chanted in the wrap-around fallopian coziness of my red Mustang, an infinitely more religious vehicle than the T-Bird I had owned in college. . . . a long journey on wheels into the slavering mouth of an incredible and restless country. I shouted as I drove, exceeded speed limits, quoted poetry and folksong.

Writing back into those days, he realizes his propaganda rôle; his narrative is full of Americans surrendering to imitative, media-controlled fantasy lives, destructively in search of 'complete self-realization', within a world super-state of 'crazed power' which reads now like a passage from *White Noise* fourteen years later:

There were many visions in the land, all fragments of the exploded dream, and some of the darkest of these visions were those processed in triplicate by our generals and industrialists—the manganese empires, the super-sophisticated gunnery, the consortiums and privileges.

He dreams of a 'junkless' life, envies a writer who experiences 'real danger', or the astronauts—something beyond 'mining the buried metals of other countries or sending the pilots of your squadrons to hang their bombs over some illiterate village'. Instead his life is 'an image made in the image and likeness of images' in a Kafka unity, and on the radio:

a never-ending squall of disc-jockey baby-talk, commercials for death, upstate blue-grass Jesus. . . . I perceived that all was harmony, the stunned land feeding the convulsive radio, every acre of the night bursting with a kinetic unity, the logic beyond delirium.

Characteristic of a nation obsessed with autobiography and biography, Bell plans a ghastly movie that 'attempts to explore parts of my consciousness. . . . Ghosts and shadows everywhere in terms of technique'—junk, in fact, but he is pleased: 'child of Godard and Coca Cola'. His woman friend Sullivan tells a real story of her sex life, at his request, but it

56

is impossible to know whether it is actual or not: 'You must permit me at least a fraction of the self-indulgence you reserve for your own tired ends.'

These characters use their over-written, over-spoken and over-visualized abilities and arts for power. Their parody of art comes from books and films, their models. Media people, as Americans have become, they define themselves by a rhetoric of voyeurism and ventriloquism. Sullivan knows her story out of Coleridge, Melville, Conrad, Faulkner, O'Neill and Joyce, an absurd cut-up of borrowings. The sexual scene with her in Chapter 11 is an elaborate 'mime of some creature that has been burrowing for centuries . . . and entering her I was occupied by her, the army occupied by the city. Abomination.' She tells him he is 'a lovable cliché'. Bell takes off into

> the depths of America, wilderness dream of all poets and scoutmasters, westward to our manifest destiny, to sovereign red timber and painted sands, to the gold-transfigured hills, westward to match the shadows of my image of myself.

His solitary end is 'self-serving research' for a book-equivalent of his film: 'I myself appear briefly at the very end, reflected in a mirror as I hold the camera.' He wanted to be an artist, but media turns art into Americana. Listening to his favourite disc-jockey Beasley, he phones him and discovers he is on tape:

> we're all on tape. All of us. . . . I felt it was literature I had been confronting these past days, the archetypes of the dismal mystery, sons and daughters of the archetypes, images that could not be certain which of two confusions held less terror, their own or what their own might become if it ever faced the truth. I drove at insane speeds.

On the way to a flight east to New York, Bell ends the American part of his life in the location towards which DeLillo's career moves in 1988—the School Book Depository, Dealey Plaza, the triple underpass of Dallas, where Americana reached a typical climax in 1963: sacrificial murder of a cultural archetype, John F. Kennedy.

Then DeLillo turned to the cult of sport, another media

racket, and Americana obsession—'Through every indicator we possess, sport and play are at present seen to consume our time and energies.' Christian Messenger's excellent book engages the issues further[5]:

> The sports hero in American fiction . . . is typically described in a series of encounters between the player and his society. While the focus is consistently on physical sport . . . the competition described often turns ironic, abstract, and metaphorical. Here the play spirit predominates in metaphors of control and loss, mastery and tragic defeat. . . . Sport in American life has always been contradictory. It liberates in play, but it binds its players to the utmost strenuous work . . . Reuel Denney stated (*The Astonished Muse*, 1957), 'In the American culture as a whole, no sharp line exists between work and play'. . . . Play and game, sport and work. The terminology is most often fluid and ambiguous in the American experience.

And the sacred and play notoriously resemble each other as unities of winning and sacrifice between sides, antagonistic spirits or gods and their priests or agents, and their religions of agencies. Messenger does not use Georges Bataille but the latter's essay, 'Sacrifice' (1933), is to the point, with its inclusions of erotic ecstasy, enclosed mimicries of order, belief in luck (prayers in the locker-room before matches are commonplace), ritual costuming, 'the revelation' and 'domination' of the *me* in personal and group existence, drugs, and so forth, in patterns of need that are simultaneously within and separate from social life.[6] Messenger cites current play theory that does not contrast 'reality', 'culture' and 'the sacred' but places it as 'an essential element of man's ontological make-up', 'a basic existential phenomenon'. DeLillo's novel is deep into the ways 'we play our reality, our work, our religion', and into the primary force of language to anchor play. In political, military and cultural institutions, too, rules and rule-breaking control those patterns of dominance and submission which are social bases, with the consequent 'loss of true, free personality'.

Messenger particularly identifies the Ritual Sports Hero, the Popular Sports Hero and the School Sports Hero that shape the American sports field in the state's rituals. The networks of *End Zone* (1972) engage sports Americana through male students studying philosophical and religious issues, developing sexual methods, and playing hard American football. They discover, what surely millions of Americans believe, that God, 'the man upstairs', is waiting for the result of the football season. At Penn State, the coach lays it on the narrator, Gary Harkness: football is a team-sport training in the need to sacrifice, a preparation for the future, a microcosm of life. While placards yelling MILITARIZE appear all over his town, Harkness reads a huge book on 'the possibilities of nuclear war', a course assignment for 'modes of disaster technology'. Like David Bell, he is overwhelmed by ritualist language of order:

> The problem was simple and terrible: I enjoyed the book. . . . I became fascinated by words and phrases like thermal hurricane, overkill, circular error probability, post-attack environment, stark deterrence, dose-rate contours, kill-ratio, spasm war. . . . New concepts appeared—the rationality of irrationality, hostage cities, orbital attacks.

He learns from Major Staley, the R.O.T.C. director, lecturer in war studies, that 'war is the ultimate realization of modern technology' and therefore the centre of value:

> For centuries men have tested themselves in war. War was the final test, the great experience, the privilege, the honour, the self-sacrifice or what have you, the absolutely ultimate determination of what kind of man you were. War was the great challenge—the great evaluator.

The rest is irrelevant, including 'the grotesque sense of patriotism at work in this country'. 'War is a test of opposing technologies.' But Alan Zapalac, instructor in exobiology, challenges another common belief: football is *not* a substitute for war; it fulfils a basic human need, but like all key rituals it incurs control by language: 'It is the one sport guided by language, by the word signal, the snap number, the colour code, the play name . . . [it] dependent on elegant gibberish.' This combined structure of words, numbers, code, names—gibberish—will control DeLillo's next novels. Meanwhile, in *End Zone* (Part 3) Wally Pippich, hired as sports information director, is a word maniac who calls shaking hands 'handation'; and Staley encourages Harkness to join the Air Force as a stage beyond football and 'the most self-actualizing branch of the military'. But Gary is out of the cold war world and listens to Zapalac voicing characteristic 1970s liberal fears of the Kennedy administration and its successors—a main motivation in *Libra*—their controllers in 'the military-industrial complex', and their electors, the propagandized masses. But even in 1972 the 1960s rebelliousness of youth against American officialdom could be a hopeful resource:

> I'm afraid of my country . . . Science fiction is just beginning to catch up with the Old Testament. See artificial nitrates run off into the rivers and oceans. See carbon dioxide melt the polar ice caps . . . See wars, famine and plague . . . see wild stallions mount the prairie dogs. I said science fiction but I guess science. Anyway there's some kind of mythical and/or historic circle-thing being completed here. But I keep smiling. I keep telling myself there's nothing to worry about as long as the youth of America knows what's going on. Brains, brawn, good teeth, tallness. . . . Some of you in your nifty blue uniforms here to learn about outer space and how to police it. Uniforms, flags, battle hymns. I offer you my only quotable remark of the entire fall semester. A nation is never more ridiculous than in its patriotic manifestations. Why should I be afraid of my own government? There's something wrong here. . . . I'm not worried. Fortunately I'm good at ducking. . . . Let's open to page seventy-eight. The panspermic hypothesis and its heartwarming implications.

Out of this unnerved parodistic credo, DeLillo will draw some of his forthcoming materials—science/science fiction interactions, futile patriotism, militarist power, the institutionalized wreckage of nature. Possibly the only use of 'paranoid' appears at this point, when Zapalac owns: 'Granted I'm a little bit paranoid. But I've got a nose for terror . . . I can hear the engine revving.' His fear is for youth trained by exactly those 'respectable parents . . . who are ripping up the forests with their engines, their money-building machines'. These kids are children of the network. But Zapalac is long ago compromised:

I love sports. I love football . . . Warfare is warfare. We don't
need substitutes because we've got the real thing. The crowds
are fantastic. They jump and scream . . . I'm crazy for it. I
wallow in it.

Gary Harkness responds: 'The real needs of man'. Zapalac's
own science fiction is deep into half-mollusc nautiloids twice
human size and communicating through an 'intricate ESP
number system'. Some 'black light' enters one of their
brains; it turns into 'a mass of equations and formulas
rendered into some kind of tangible form'.

The God-watched football season, monolithic government,
hidden state controls and the interlocking of science and its
fictional myths—the subject area of *Ratner's Star* (1976)—
draw together in the thing's ability to make endless like-
nesses and words for them, and 'then delivering the words
into its own circuitry'. It is a 'monadanom' embodying total
cosmos, total generation, an 'everything figure'—an organization which is parodied in *Libra* as a Joycean C.I.A. assem-
bler of endless information about the Kennedy assassination.
Sensibly, DeLillo breaks off Zapalac's fiction here. He will
have more fun with Leibnizean monads later as the dire
needs of man. Meanwhile the games and languages continue
their web system. The coach, Emmett Creed, explains from
his wheelchair: 'a complex of systems . . . an interlocking
number of systems . . . brutal only from a distance. In the
middle of it there's a calm, a tranquility . . . there's a harmony.' To be a unit within it is high sacrificial value—'pain
is part of the harmony of the nervous system.' Creed sees
Harkness as a future leader and confers the post of 'offensive
captain' on him. Immediately Gary goes into an American
nervousness on leadership and superiority within an ostensibly democratic system:

> I became depressed. No American accepts the deputy's badge
> without misgivings; centuries of heroic lawlessness have cap-
> tured our blood. I felt responsible for a vague betrayal of some
> local code or lore. I was never part of the apparatus . . . Now
> I was the law's small tin glitter.

This constellation of order in *Libra* draws in both the
C.I.A. and Lee Harvey Oswald the Marxist, both ambivalent

about state controls, both hysterical with need for network. Another preview of *Ratner's Star* is afforded in the student Bloomberg's imagining 'an anguished physicist' with his 'super-megaroach aerosol bomb which can kill anything that moves on the whole earth in a fraction of a microsecond and which I alone invented and marketed'. T.V. crews dog him into 'the peaceful country lanes of the Institute for Abstract Speculation and Sneak Attacks'. Now Harkness is drawn into Staley's war games, precedent scenarios of 'joyous visions of apocalypse'. One student, Taft, opts out of 'the pattern, the morality' imposed by Creed—'part Satan, part Saint Francis or somebody'—but Harkness ends in the infirmary, fed 'through plastic tubes'. Americana can cause total breakdown in the confused dissident.

DeLillo's following network of propaganda, an Americana area central to the 1960s and 1970s, is the rock music racket. *Great Jones Street* (1973) is narrated by a dissenting once key member, Bucky Wunderlick, ex- 'hero of rock 'n' roll', as he announces on the first page. A national hero, that is, and the American pattern is clear from this West Coast session:

> The country's blood was up, this or that atrocity, home or abroad, and even before we hit the stage the whole place was shaking. We were the one group that people depended on to validate their emotions and this was to be a night of above average fury. In our special context we challenged the authenticity of the crowd's passion and wrath, dipping our bodies in coquettish blue light, merely teasing our instruments for the first hour or so. Then caved their heads with about twenty thousand watts of frozen sound. The pressure of their response was immense, blasting in with the force of a natural disaster, and it became even greater, more physically menacing. . . .

As his manager Globke's assistant, Hanes, grasps it: 'The underground's come up with a superdrug . . . The news leaves me cold frankly. Music is the final hypnotic . . . Music is dangerous so many ways.' The rock-football-money-propaganda-drug-religiosity network is wide open for investigation:

> today, wherever there is music, there is money. . . . Music, an immaterial pleasure turned commodity, now heralds a society

of the sign, of the immaterial up for sale, of the social relation unified in money.

Jacques Attali then characterizes the chart-system as a way of perceiving 'a society of repetition' fetishizing 'the multiplication of semi-identified objects'. This power is 'strategic and military', another programming of the mass by network and commercials, and deeply reliant on religious or dionysian rites, as well as propaganda, or the political economy of imposed order. As David Bell concludes on his remote island, and Gary Harkness moves into his peculiar 'end zone', so Bucky Wunderlick reaches 'endland, far from the tropics of fame', a seedy downtown New York street apartment.

Attali identifies three 'zones' of music power, where people are trained to forget silence, believe in harmony (like Creed and Staley), and to be silent by deafening and censorship. Their methods are ritual sacrifice, representation and repetition—the network programming of *Americana*. But whereas Attali believes this is subversive, DeLillo more accurately understands it as part of the systematics of authority, utilized it is assumed to be the real needs of man. His interior plot, carried through the next novels and into *Libra*, is: may be they are. Attali believes that the pop-rock network is 'a way of filling the absence of meaning in the world. It creates a system of apolitical, nonconflictual, idealized values.'[7] DeLillo enquires further—as he has begun to in his first two novels—into the star-system, the separations of fame, the sacrificial games of ostensible democracy. Wunderlick looks back from experience, and enters the field of Bataille's examinations of excess:

> Fame requires every kind of excess . . . I mean danger, the edge of every void, the circumstance of one man imparting an erotic terror to the dreams of the republic. Understand the man who must inhabit these extreme regions, monstrous and vulval, damp with memories of violation. Even if half-mad he is absorbed into the public's contempt for survivors. . . . Perhaps the only natural law attaching to true fame is that the famous man is compelled, eventually, to commit suicide.

At this climactic point, Bucky opts out, and understands— beyond Attali—'our audience wanted more than music more even than its own reduplicated noise. . . . Our followers . . . were less murderous in their love of me', that 'Me' which Bataille detects in ritual existence. Their silent mimicking of the band marked the end: 'Either I'd return with a new language for them to speak or they'd seek a divine silence attendant on my own.' The previous night the police had enjoyed 'the feast' of audience-breaking—'they made their patented charges, cracking arms and legs in an effort to protect the concept of regulated temperature.' Globke calls it 'an example of mini-genocide'. But the group is part of his own network, Transparanoia—a name invented by Wunderlick—which also owns the Great Jones Street building to which Bucky has retreated.[8] Four days after escape he is visited by a reporter from RUNNING DOG NEWS SERVICE, and decides, 'You decide . . . Whatever you write will be true. I'll confirm every word.' His other visitors include Fenig, a writer for whatever the market demands, and a salesman (Dr. Pepper, the master genius, in one of his disguises), peddling 'selected brushes made by handicapped ex-fighting men'—'Iwo Jima, Corregidor, Salerno, Belleau Wood, Bataan, back to Bataan, Iwo Jima, Paris, Norway'. As Hanes's credo is 'People use me for whatever they want. It's my way of existing', so Fenig: 'The big wheel . . . the market . . . Fame'. Most marketable is 'the ultimate drug', stolen by the Happy Valley Farm Commune from a U.S. government top-secret installation and therefore 'bound to be a real mind-crusher. . . . People are agog. It's the dawning of the age of God knows what.' Happy Valley needs to consult Dr. Pepper, 'the scientific genius of the underground'. Its aim is allegedly freedom through privacy,' the only way to destroy the notion of mass man. . . . Revolutionary solitude. Turn inward one and all . . . Sustain your privacy with aggressive self-defense.'

DeLillo's 'takes' on the 1960s 'underground' rackets—both governmental and dissident—are augmented by Bucky's companion, Opel, recalling a track star in Dakar using 'some nothing dope. Whatever athletes use'. She realizes that the drug network is a version of religion—for her, back to a Baptist immersion ritual when she was five or six: 'I was drowned.' Sex also augments the need: 'a moral form to master commerce,' Bucky takes it, 'the bodies we were and the danger we needed, that of dredging each other's insufficiencies'. Meanwhile, official business continues. The Morehouse Professor of Latent History at the Ormond Institute (Dr. Pepper): 'Latent history never tells us where we stand in the sweep of events but rather how we can get out of the way.' Zenko Alataki at work on artificial earthquakes: 'the greatest work of art ever achieved. Except we don't call it art.' And many more in Part 3 of the book. Opel knows the effect on human life of this system of degrading experimentation, including rock and drugs and pseudo-communes: 'I'm luggage . . . I open myself up, insert some very costly items and then close up again.' It shortly closes her for ever.

DeLillo includes parodies of interviews, fan stories, news reports and rock lyrics that support the racket, and a seminar of Chance Mainway Publications and the Issues Committee of the Permanent Symposium for the Restoration of Democratic Options. Bucky's guest speech works in Attali's field:

> That's why we're so great. We make noise. . . . You have to crush people's heads. That's the only way to make those fuckers listen. . . . I'd like to injure people with sound. Maybe actually kill some of them.

This is in fact one more Transparanoia package. The Wunderlick group's leader, Azarian, would include the blackness network, through which DeLillo parodies the packaged mysticism of blackness in the heyday of rock: a white noisemaker using 'black is the baddest in the best sense . . . the weightiest of all trips.' The 'media leeches'—their own term—move in because: 'People want words and pictures . . . Your power grows. The less you say, the more you are.' Globke appeals to Wunderlick to return: 'America is out there . . . it's full of people waiting to be told what to do. . . . this is a pivotal time in the music business and in the future of the country as a whole.' The way back is through some unreleased tapes with acoustic guitar—'genuinely infantile . . . cheap plastic tricks . . . full of repetition, mistakes and slurred words', appropriate for the fans—'their fear in baby bottles under their seats'. The whole system is summarized by Dr. Pepper, one of DeLillo's manic power advisers:

> What is US Guv? . . . It's big business, big army and big government all visiting each other in company planes for the sole purpose of playing golf and talking money. So who does that leave in positions of trust? Friends, it leaves you and me.

Dr. Pepper is DeLillo's representative of powerful illegality, a confidence man whose centre is the ultimate drug, the real need of man—a need which will be extended and deepened in *Running Dog* and *The Names*: 'Everybody in the free world to bid. There's a group on the Coast wants to bid . . . Great Britain and Europe . . . I crave new frontiers.' He is Control, named after a famous American bottled drink, a version of Fu Manchu, Faust, Dracula, Dr. Strangelove, Volpone and many others in the history of fiction, created out of real need:

> Energy is the power of the universe. I want to tap that power. I see masses of people changing their energy patterns by controlling bio-rhythms from the basic frequencies of the universe . . . Control of internal changes. I envisage abuses, of course . . . Cures of cancer in seconds! Adds inches to your cock! . . . a technical and merchandizing feat that goes beyond the legendary . . . I call the process centrifugalism. Stereo electrodes. Blood-pressure impactors. What I call the auto-domination of the inner mind.

In other words, a grandiose extension of Azarian's 'Keep the public salivating.' And its basis is a 'US Guv' drug to silence dissidence. Bohack of Happy Valley also needs to control 'mindless violence' in 'a runaway continent'. As an ex-college football jock and a victim of noise, he can draw the system together: 'violence without historical weight is basically faggot violence and basically ludicrous.' But his attitudes towards Bucky are ambivalent: 'we were willing victims of your sound. Now we're acolytes of your silence.' One of the 'baby bottle' lyrics is clear enough— another example of gibberish control: 'Nothing-maker/ But to blurt/ But to sing/ Baby god and goo'. Bohack owns a pack of 'dog-boys' to do his work and will use them unless Bucky fulfils his mission in suicide in 'some mysterious or remote place . . . the final inward plunge, Bucky. It's what you owe us.' The drug will enter him: 'You'll be perfectly healthy. You won't be able to make words, that's all. They just won't come into your mind . . . Sounds galore. But no words. No songs.' Wunderlick cooperates: 'Several weeks of immense serenity'. Rumours include 'living among beggars and syphilitics, performing good works, patron saint of all those men who hear the river-whistles sing the mysteries'. Media gibberish wins again.

The verbalisms of network in *Ratner's Star* are part of a 430-page satire on the needs of science producers complying with and trying to resist the political-technological system. Television, football, rock music and the underground, and now in 1976, the year of its publication, a further addition to DeLillo's encyclopaedia of need. This time he requires a third-person narrative to hold the huge network of engineering, mathematics and logic. The main performer is a 14-year-old first Nobel laureate in mathematics, Billy Twillig, officially employed to decode an alleged radio message from a star. Within the establishment set up for this and concomittant research, the participants discover their organizational rôles and the limits of their creativity. The core mystique is numbers. Only three or four people understand Billy's discovery—a class of numbers called zorgs. He needs numbers as a way of life:

> How did it go? *Aš min eš limmu ia aš imin ussu ilimmu u.* Ever one more number, individual and distinct, fixed in place, absolutely whole . . . Pre-cuneiform. Marked with tapered stylus on clay slabs. Number as primitive intuition. Number self-generated. Number developing in the child's mind spontaneously and nonverbally. . . . He calculated with the ease of a coastal bird haunting an updraft . . . adhering strictly to a set of consistent inner codes, and this he clearly perceived, the arch-reality of pure mathematics. . . . the manifold freedom it offers in the very strictures it persistently upholds.

One hundred nations share the cost of the installation. One group of researchers sit 'in a kind of triangular pattern studied in depth by early believers in the self-hood of numbers. What was ten was also four, triangle and password, *tetraktys*, hold fourfoldness.' The mathematician and astrophysicist

Henrik Endor—his name says why he wears a star penta-
gram on a chain round his neck—failed to 'find a pattern' in
the assumed code from Ratner's star message. May be there
is no pattern. Field Experiment No. 1 therefore investigates
behaviour changes, involved in all networks: its aim—'We
can discover the truth or falsehood of our own final designs
only if we teach ourselves to think as a single planetary
mind.' Endor, now living in a hole in the earth, summons
Twillig to ask him the key question, a question that in fact
haunts DeLillo's fictions increasingly: 'If all matter possesses
one nature and seeks to unite with all other matter, why are
things flying apart?' Seeking unity, 'we deny the evidence
of our senses. I'm tired of denying such evidence. . . . If
the moon and sun cause tides in oceans, why don't they
cause tides in pools and glasses of water?' He warns Billy
that the 'dark side' of the Ratner message is that it may tell
us about ourselves. Endor sacrificed himself and is now able
to diagnose his exemplary condition:

> Loneliness among the over-educated is the saddest thing in
> the world. . . . My work here is interdisciplinary. This is the
> loneliest kind of work. . . . Living defensively is the central
> theme of our age . . . the only way to survive is to curtail
> perspective, to exist as close to one's centre as possible.

As for the network: 'There is always a higher authority than
you think.' DeLillo is investigating the manic need for origins
and interpretations of the ultimate. Science is *the* game, and
Endor's advice is endemic: 'Never misuse the freedom to
invent.' After failure, he 'cursed science and the natural
limits of man'; now his pleasures are finger-counting and
'nonverbal sounds'. Number is endless need and pleasure in
his end zone, against dread. Old Ratner is kept alive by doc-
tors and nurses, a zone of 'corporate names, brand names,
slogans and symbols' specializing in complex medical engineering. His ceremonial speech in Chapter 10 concerns creation origin, a huge explanation of total process assumed to
be the work of G-dash-D. The Word interprets everything
beyond hidden essence, a truth beneath the truth. The
whole rigmarole is stultifyingly religious inside which Billy
is a mere golem, 'an artificial person'. His remedy would

be to enter Ratner's semitic mysticism—he has contacted *en-sof*, the Kabbalah infinity, 'the hidden dynamic' of divine life found in 'every realm of creation . . . the hidden root . . . never manifested, not even in symbols'. The Hebrew alphabet 'which sprang from the inner linguistic movement of *en-sof*' is 'spun' from the immanent 'beatitude' pervading *en-sof*, 'the infinite, beginningless and uncreated'.[9]

Billy bypasses such games and declares the transmission a number. The first half of its problem is solved without the 'extra-mathematical context of mathematics'. The signal is repeated. Bill confronts Logik, an alternative maths, and feels sick knowing this is 'symbolic notation itself'. Robert Softly proposes 'a logistic cosmic language based on mathematical principles', 'precise ideographic symbols'. Part 2 is called 'Logician Project Minus-One'. The project becomes increasingly abstract from forms of personal need, fuelled by 'the human demonology of love', resisting 'mounting international tension'. Deep under the installation, the 'supersavants' work in a version of Bohack's 'absolute privacy', working largely on a parodistic version of Noam Chomsky's universal grammar, of Korzybski's studies in logic, and Kafka's unity:

> History . . . has no worthwhile statement to make to us, however, in our current preoccupation. We're permitted to deduce, at least at the outset, that everything is either *a* or non-*a*. What we're not permitted to do is say that everything is either the Great Wall of China or something else. In our present circumstances we don't even know the Great Wall exists. We've never heard of it. So let's forget about history.

The result is Logicon, an interstellar vocabulary; work on it is, like football, a sacrificial discipline—Lester Bolin suggests uniforms, in fact, 'team jerseys with LOGICON sewed across the front', signs of 'splendid *Einheit* or unity'. But then he is a linguistic who says 'laughter' instead of actually laughing. Sex becomes 'secret language', 'erotic language', which interferes with Billy's need for energy with 'no sequential meaning . . . no real process of thought and repetition . . . no organized content . . . essentially unteachable'. Maurice Wu only needs to believe that 'layer by layer there is evidence of greater complexity'. Jean Venables states the fact that the Project is—like any other system—liable to be 'a game . . . with specific rules that govern every operation'. Edna Lown finds happiness in its *'holism, a state of unqualified being'*. Chester Greylag Dent helps Softly invent a logical language built into computer-driven machinery 'able to speak about itself in metalogical terms'. The illusion of all network systems is the same: the illusion of actually producing fact. DeLillo probes desire for ideological and technological completion, rife in Americana and in the proliferations of post-modernist schematology or 'techniques of destiny'. He probes, too, the dehumanized symbol mania of computerology and the real needs of its fanatic promoters. No wonder Softly looks at his semen and hates it as 'a reaction (perhaps) to danger or excessive stress'; sex is, after all, 'balance of sag and nonsag in egg-shaped structures'.

But Billy discovers, through a Coca-Cola clock, that Endor had in fact 'cracked the star code'. It makes little difference. Wu plunges into 'reverse evolution . . . advancement backward', and wails in panic—nonverbal sounds. DeLillo changes the scene to India for an *unexpected* eclipse of the sun, and concludes with a range of religious network origins and practices. Soul is everywhere passing through soul, going in and out of frames of logic:

> Having dismantled the handiwork of your own perceptions in order to solve reality, you know it now as a micron flash of light-scattering matter in a structure otherwise composed of purely mathematical coordinates.

A Vedantic text, originating in India, is 'a printed seed of the race', 'the source of positional notation for the decimal system and of the symbols for the numbers one to nine'. India is the location of networks: 'lifelong celibates', poverty, beggary and the 'audible drone of sacred names, as everywhere, all the plain-weave variations of supplicatory noise'—everywhere including Great Jones Street. At whatever cost and absurdity, man needs 'the prolongation of order'. Billy is last seen pedalling madly on his white tricycle in 'a white area' preceding total eclipse, laughing his nonverbal sounds, entering *his* endland, escaped into transience.

By page 100 of *Players* (1977), Lyle Wynant already experiences the characteristic disengagement from his contingent life that DeLillo's exemplary figures suffer. A sense of mere game assails him:

> He was slipping right through. A play . . . He found himself bored, often, at the theatre (although never at movies . . .). This kind of tropor was generated by three-dimensional bodies, real space as opposed to the manipulated depth of film.

To Kinnear, who will recruit him to an underground movement, he reveals the white-collar network member's dream of power:

> To place a call from a public booth in the middle of the night. Calling some government bureau, some official department, right, of the government. 'I have information about so-and-so.' Or, even better, to be visited, to have them come to you. . . . 'You might be willing to provide a recruiter with cover on your payroll, sir.' Imagine how sexy that can be for the true-blue business man or professor. What an incredible night-time thrill. The appeal of mazes and intricate techniques. The suggestion of a double life.

Kinnear operates a field which DeLillo will develop extensively in *The Names* and *Libra*:

> I operate on basic, really visceral levels. Terror is purification. When you set out to rid a society of repressive elements, you immediately become a target yourself, for all sorts of people. . . . Being killed or betrayed, sometimes seems the point of it all.

Lyle replaces George Sedbauer, who did 'business with the other side', 'hanging around with the wild-eyed radicals, with the bomb-throwers', believing he worked for

> high-level—quote—industrial espionage—close quote. We led him to believe we represented international banking and shipping interests. . . . It never occurred to him until the end, literally the last minute, I would think, that Vilar wanted to blow up the Exchange.

DeLillo's new field of permissive innocence is, central to late twentieth-century political action, the terrorist organization. But, once again, this is part of fascination with 'the thing hideously behind', a phrase in Henry James's *The*

Golden Bowl—and in the preface to *The American,* James writes of the interplay of 'things we cannot possibly *not* know' and 'things that we *can* never directly know', perceived through 'circuit and subterfuge of our thought and desire'. (Both James and Conrad wrote novels using anarchist terror.) Within these schemes, erotic will loves to masquerade as permissive need, as peculiar a need for 'performance' play, as DeLillo offers in Chapter 3 of Part 1:

> She brought him back, needing the contact of surfaces, the palpable logic of his cock inside her. Then she was gripping hard, released to the contagion of recurring motion, rising, as they ached and played, sunny as young tigers.
>
> It is time to 'perform', he thought. She would have to be 'satisfied'. He would have to 'service' her. They would make efforts to 'interact'.

Sex becomes self-conscious theatre or movie, just as terrorism does under treatment by television. DeLillo begins with 'A Movie', film-script silent visuals, non-verbal 'routine', to be interpreted, the audience as 'privileged onlookers', in which terrorists invade a golf-course of players:

> To the glamour of revolutionary violence, to the secret longing it evokes in the most docile soul, the piano's shiny tinkle brings an irony too apt to be ignored . . . undermines the photogenic terror. . . . History this weightless has an easy time of it, we learn, contending with the burdens of the present day.

So Bohack's words in *Great Jones Street* return in another context, and the issue is again sacrifice: 'The terrorist chief, *jefe*, honcho, leader fires several rounds into the air—a blood rite or passionate declaration. Buster Keaton, says the piano.' Or Woody Allen's perceptive satire six years earlier in *Bananas*. Lyle can reduce a shooting at the Exchange, where he works, to a cheap movie, for conversation with his wife:

> I wouldn't want to say porta rickens. I wouldn't want to say coloured or any of the well-meaning white folks who have taken up the struggle, not knowing, you see, that the capitalist system and the pattern of repression are themselves a struggle. It's not an easy matter being an oppressor. . . .

Then he himself is picked up by Marina Vilar and finds himself in 'a play', a network attack the network of 'US

Guv' and the Exchange. Kinnear makes the point, basic for the C.I.A./F.B.I. convolutions in *Libra*—Americana's official terrorist system, part of the pattern of Noam Chomsky's exposure, *The Culture of Terrorism*, also published in 1988:

> It's everywhere isn't it? Mazes, you're correct. Intricate techniques. Our big problem in the past, as a nation, is that we didn't give our government credit for being the totally entangling force that it was. They were even more evil than we'd imagined. More evil and much more interesting. Assassination, blackmail, torture, enormous improbable intrigues. All these convolutions and relationships. Assorted sexual episodes . . . We thought they bombed villages, killed children, for the sake of technology, as it could shake itself out, and for certain abstractions. . . . Behind every stark fact we encounter layers of ambiguity. . . . This haze of conspiracies and multipile interpretations. So much for the great instructing vision of the federal government. . . . Why were the papers shredded and what did they say? . . . Who erased the tapes? . . . How did organized crime get involved—who let *them* in? How deeply are the corporations involved in this or that mystery, this or that crime, these murders, these programmes of systematic torture? Who ordered these massive surveillance programmes? . . . Why did these witnesses drop out of sight? . . . Where are the missing bullet fragments? Did this suspect work for the intelligence service or didn't he? . . . What happened, Lyle, on the floor that day?

In Chomsky's words: 'The state must spin an elaborate web of illusion and deceit, with the co-operation of ideological institutions that generally serve its interests.'[10] The state *is* network violence, and therefore target of Kinnear's organization, focussed on the Exchange. His account of the state reads like part of *Ratner's Star*:

> Their system, the idea of world-wide money. It's that *system* that we believe is their secret power . . . Currents of invisible life. This is the centre of their existence. The electronic system. The waves and charges. The green numbers on the board. . . . their way of continuing on through the rotting flesh, their closest taste of immortality.

Terrorist action is essential against 'Eleven Wall' therefore: a real need against real power games. But the state, the

Kinnear system, and Lyle and his wife Pammy, are also in erotic need of feeling themselves inside drama, the illusions of being psyched-up into changed selves. Pammy leaves for Maine to play with two homosexuals: 'You wanted drama, right? A change.' Inside the organization Lyle had 'never felt so *intelligent* before', and his thrill is completed when his dream is realized when the other side contact him—through one, Burks. Like many of DeLillo's figures, and especially the agency men and Lee Harvey Oswald in *Libra*, Lyle is energized by a sense of historicization, a main feature of permissive innocence at its most virulent. He is wandering through monied New York at night:

> An occult theology of money, extending ever deeper into its own veined marble. . . . At its inmost crypt might be heard the amplitude pulse of history, a system and a rite to outshadow the evidence of men's senses.

Pammy enters the dangers of 'new places'—a feature in *The Names*—'too much feedback that's not pre-determined' —and 'a whole era of things' she missed out on in the Village '60s, summarized in pseudo-Beat media terms: 'Whatever feels right, as long as you both want to do it and nobody gets hurt, there's no reason not to. . . . Follow your instincts, be yourself, act out your fantasies.' That is, the obverse side of what all systems and the permissiveness encourage. Meanwhile Lyle comes across an actual oppression—he reads a pamphlet distributed by a man outside Federal Hall on the real oppression of workers of the world since 1850. DeLillo edges the novel nearer *Libra*: 'a little razzle-dazzle in New Orleans, late spring in sixty-three . . . some lawyer attached to a government committee . . . connections, funny under-currents. Oswald, for instance. Cuba, for instance.' When Kinnear surfaces in the cocaine system in Bogotà, we are in the future of *Miami Vice,* a main political education resource for American masses in the 1980s.

But Lyle's talent relates him to a number of DeLillo's victims of intrigue: 'He had a feel for numbers. . . . He'd developed ways to remember, methods that went back to early adolescence . . . secret mnemonic devices.' He is eminently usable in the late twentieth century, and he

also 'loves secret currents'. He has to ask Kinnear if in
fact he knew Oswald before Dallas. Kinnear replies: 'Lyle,
chrissake, everybody knew Oswald before Dallas.' The 'clan-
destine life', 'enmeshed in a psychology of stealth', the life
of transience and motels—a basis of *Running Dog*—lurches
forward. Back in New York, Pammy sees a flophouse sign
that reads 'TRANSIENTS . . . seconds passed before she
grasped its meaning.' Lyle's end zone is a motel room where
he imagines

> that this vast system of nearly identical rooms, worldwide,
> has been established so that people will have somewhere to be
> *afraid* on a regular basis. The parings of our various researches.
> Somewhere to take our fear.

But this section is a movie complementing the opening
one: 'The Motel'. Lyle tries to 'pull things into a systematic
pattern or the illusion of a systematic pattern. Numbers are
but for this.' As he awaits a masterful female with a dildo,
his endland is completed:

> The propped figure, for instance, is barely recognizable as
> male. Shedding capabilities and traits by the second he can
> still be described (but quickly) as well-formed, sentient and
> fair. We know nothing else about him.

Network drains individuality into its parasitic numbers and
controls; the yielder vanishes into the host megastructure,
becomes its transient, placeless, sacrificed, part of reasons
of state or any other manifestation of Control. James Axton
exists in a 'world of corporate transients' and, like Lyle,
Twillig, Bell and others through to Oswald, becomes a used
operative in a predatory system. This time, in *The Names*, his
finest novel so far (1983), DeLillo counters with an alternative life, just as obsessive in its needs but less dangerously
nourishing and similar to that crucial sense in Fitzgerald's
fictions, exemplified in Dick Diver's cry in *Tender is the
Night* (1934), 'Have I been nourished?', and expressed in
one of the 'crack-up' essays of 1936 as the loss of 'the ability
to function' through the loss of a belief that 'you were
never going to have the power of a man of strong political
convictions but you were certainly more independent.'[11] The

nourisher in *The Names* is Owen Brademas, archeologist and anthropologist. Axton's wife, Kathryn, and their 9-year-old son, Tap, have joined his dig in Greece, on Kouros, in search of something beyond transience and corporate network—but still instigated by the urge towards origins, and possibly monadic origins.

Axton works in 'risk analysis', an executive for multinational corporations, part of a peculiarly late twentieth-century pattern:

> . . . a subculture, business people in transit, growing old in planes and airports . . . We were versed in percentages, safety records, in the humour of flaming death. . . . We knew the various aircraft and their configurations and measured this against the distances we were flying. . . . We advised each other on which remote cities were well maintained, which were notable for wild dogs running in packs at night, snipers in the business district at high noon. . . . We knew where martial law was in force, where body searches were made, where they engaged in systematic torture, or fired assault rifles in the air at weddings, or abducted and ransomed executives. This was the humour of personal humiliation. . . . Nothing sticks to us but smoke in our hair and clothes.

In this world of petrodollars in places of 'plastic sandals and public beheadings', Axton's life is devoid of differentiation and of value through distinction: 'I go everywhere twice. Once to get the wrong impression, once to strengthen it.' But simultaneously active is an organization counter to the pseudo-order of executive transience and world currency investment, a small network for ritual sacrificial murder. DeLillo's fascination now entertains a system whose methods appear to be fanatically arbitrary: the killers match the initials of crippled, decayed villages with those of their victims' towns and names. The real need of man reaches into a level of human necessity for order and power, beyond the motivations in the previous novels. In Brademas's words: 'We thought we knew this setting. The mass killer in his furnished room, in his century, feeding Gaines Burgers to his German shepherd . . . Men firing from highway overpasses, attic rooms.' But this *acte gratuit*—for DeLillo is working in this twentieth-century field—is based on a fetishism of sign, part of human obsession with alphabet and number, fundamental and atavistic, beyond law and therapy. The network stretches throughout that area of Greece, the Middle East and India, where world religion, and written languages and the systematics of number, originate. Or so it is believed. The West has long ago moved in with its own religion and its mystique: 'Technicians are the infiltrators of ancient societies. They speak a secret language. They bring new kinds of death with them.' But they also use the world's languages for their own power. In Chapter 9 of *Great Jones Street*: 'too much travel simply isolates people. It narrows them.' In *The Names* Americans travel to extend American control as well as in need of their own transience. Axton analyses killings and enslavements, for various reasons and none at all, controls for their advantages of pleasure with assumed permissions:

> America is the world's living myth. There's no sense of wrong when you kill an American or blame America for some local disaster. . . . Whatever people need, we provide. A myth is a useful thing . . . There must be times when a society feels the purest virtue lies in killing.

Axton initially bypasses the Acropolis: 'It's what we've rescued from the madness. Beauty, dignity, order, proportion. There are obligations attached to such a visit.' Now he visits a culture to 'review the political and economic situation . . . whatever endangers investment', and finds himself surrounded by tourism: 'the march of stupidity'. Brademas digs into the past of the area, into the Minoan code of law written as *boustrophedon*, reading stone inscriptions, learning Sanskrit, studying pavement mosaics, alphabets:

> Religion. People driven by the same powerful emotion. All that reverence, awe and dread . . . Correctness of detail . . . The shapes of their letters and the materials they used. Fire-hardened clay, dense black basalt, marble with a ferous content . . . So strange and reawakening. It goes deeper than conversations, riddles.

Brademas's extreme opposite is Axton's boss, Rowser, who

has three identities, and an office in Washington 'with a letter-bomb detector, a voice scrambler, an elaborate system to prevent break-ins'—a life

> full of the ornaments of paranoia and deception. Even his hoarse voice, a forced whisper, seemed a comic symptom of the clandestine environment. . . . He sold insurance to other businessmen. The subjects were money, politics and force . . . Rowser's ultra-secure briefcase sat next to him in the soft chair. . . . Facts on the infra-structure. Probabilities, statistics. These were the music of Rowser's life, the only coherence he needed. . . . He had a gift for numbers and a temperament that enabled him to separate mathematical techniques and actuarial science from the terrifying events he culled from his figures. In the universities and research centres he attended any number of conferences at which people discussed such choice calamities as reactor meltdowns, runaway viruses and three-day spasm wars. . . . He was no game theorist or geo-politician. He had no system of assumptions and principles. What he had was a set of interlocking facts he'd drawn from tons of research material on the cost-effectiveness of terror.
>
> There had been over five thousand terrorist incidents in the past decade.
>
> Kidnappings were routine business. . . .
>
> Business executives were prime targets.
>
> US executives led the world, being targeted with particular frequency in the Middle East and Latin America.
>
> Simple. He convinced a medium-sized insurance company to sell ransom policies to the multinationals. His job was to figure the risk of enrolling applicants for coverage. . . .
>
> The man of narrow outlook becomes immersed. Rowser occupied himself profoundly in the customs and attitudes of the secret life. His thoroughness was compulsive and regenerative, a pathological condition. . . .
>
> By this time Rowser was head of development for the North-west Group, a subsidiary of a two-billion-dollar conglomerate referred to as 'the parent'.

The Names delineates the place of both Brademas and Rowser, as well as the alphabetic assassination cult, as interlocking versions of fundamental needs—in Brademas's terms, which are staple throughout DeLillo's work: 'how far men will go to satisfy a pattern, or find a pattern, or fit together the elements of a pattern'. Deciphering alphabets may be a harmless aspect but 'the scientific face of imperialism' has frequently been to 'subdue and codify'. As for the murder cult: 'certainly human sacrifice isn't new in Greece.' In Chapter 4, DeLillo introduces a version of David Bell—Frank Volterra: New York School for Private Detectives, New York University film school, maker of short films for technocrats including one on an Axton script. Now he is respected enough to generate 'reckless loyalties', and desires to work on the cult as a repetition of human need—'maybe their god is a mental defective.' Brademas places this desire in the need of twentieth-century writers for madness— 'a final distillation of self, a final editing down. It's the drowning out of false voices.' Both Axton and Volterra are interested, therefore, in 'homicidal calculation', the 'logic' in the murder cult, something unsafe. Through a guide, Vosdanik, the cult is located. Initials of the victim are carved into the murder blade, but Aramaic itself is sounds—so this is 'a religion that carries a language'—the language of Jesus—and Axton relates it to old westerns: 'If one of those bullets has your name on it, Cody, there's not a goldarned thing you can do about it.' He is so caught in the network of 'initials, names, places' that he notes: 'Jebel Amman/James Axton'. He is in Amman.

Brademas's need for investigating pattern draws him into the cult—'Elements falling into place . . . A shape in the chaos of things . . . an outer state that works somewhat the way the mind does but without the relentlessness, the predeterminate quality'. So the three men are attracted to the cult: 'the anthropologist, the storyteller, the mad logician'. DeLillo participates in all three. Volterra believes the cult will take part in his film: 'The whole world is on film, all the time. Spy satellites, microscopic scanners. . . .' He recalls the Manson family—except that this time 'these people are monks, they're secular monks. They want to vault into eternity.' The obsessive need, here and throughout DeLillo, is given in a lengthy statement by the cult member with whom the Americans liaise, Andahl. It is closely and unnervingly conscious, educated and complete:

Something in our method finds a home in your unconscious mind. A recognition . . . something you cannot analyse. We are working at a preverbal level, although we use words, of course. . . . We have in common that first experience, among others . . . of knowing this programme reaches something in us, of knowing we all wanted to be part of it. . . . Extreme, insane, whatever you wish to call it in words. Numbers behave, words do not. I knew I was right. Inevitable, perfect, and right. . . . The letters matched. . . . Something else totally. Some terrible and definitive thing. . . . Shatter his skull, kill him, smash his brains . . . nothing else would suffice. . . . You know it intuitively. . . . We are here to carry out the pattern. You have the word in English. Abecedarian . . . Lovers of the alphabet. Beginners.

The cult's name is secret because then 'the power and influence are magnified. A secret name is a way of escaping the world. It is an opening into the self.' Volterra's film, Axton's book, and DeLillo's book, are adjuncts to the need for design and its set in language and numbers, through which the preverbal is enacted. The game is watched by God; the centre is *en-sof*, and, in *The Names*, the cult mystery—the nonverbal in *Great Jones Street*. Creativity and destruction become one at this point, the mystery in, for instance, Chapter 4 of Paul Feyerabend's *Farewell to Reason* and Chapter 18 of Rupert Sheldrake's *The Presence of the Past*.[12] What appears to be power and meaning is in fact an absence: 'it's psychic grip' is 'no sense, no content, no historic bond, no ritual significance'. Design murder, manic language, god hunting, and mad multinationals interlock:

> This was the period after the President ordered a freeze of Iranian assets held in US banks. . . . The Shi'ite underground movement . . . stockpiling weapons in the Gulf . . . car bombings in Nablus and Ramallah. . . . the human noise, the heat of a running crowd . . . We all take each other's money.

The American implication of the novel is explicit: 'interesting how the Americans choose strategy over principle every time and yet keep believing in their own innocence'. And transience of sexuality again seethes within instabilities. The cult and pattern-ridden world of networks must have victims to prove its innocence. Global similarity and transience are replacing home and nation as the modern way. Reality is systems control without a fixed address: 'the world is here, the world is where I want to be.' The cult is exemplary: it is based nowhere. Kinnear's terrorist transience and illegal dealing is universally realized. At base is a human need—in Bademas's words, as he searches India, especially for Sanskrit origins: 'what was it about the letter-shapes that struck his soul with the force of a tribal mystery? . . . the secret aspect, the priestly, the aloof, the cruel.' The key question throughout the book, for all the transients and cultists is: 'how many languages do you speak?' In fact a key man in the cult is named Avtar Singh—'he suspected this was a pseudonym.' DeLillo's novel, then, is a display of avatars and atavistic needs. Towards the conclusion he includes a collection of origins for the word-idea of *book*. Singh is 'electric, messianic, crazy', the latest killer through logic and symbol obsession. For him, India, as for so many of his kind, is not a class and caste-ridden mess of poverty and religions but 'the right brain of the world': that is, the location of DeLillo's fascination with spatial skills, holistic information as distinct from analytical processes of sequentiality. Avtar Singh summarizes DeLillo's figures who desire and achieve self-referentiality through total system membership: 'The world has become self-referring. . . . How do we say the simplest thing without falling into a trap?' Questions of meaning fall back into a network without the self being otherwise satisfied. Axton concludes: 'My life is going by and I can't get a grip on it. . . . The cult is the only thing I seem to connect with.' Brademas realizes that his language mania was instilled in Kansas, as an innocent boy, from a young preacher who took Paul's 'men can speak with the tongues of angels' literally. But cult murder is not innocent, it is a dangerous mockery of the human 'need to structure and classify, to build a system against the terror in our souls. They make the system equal to the terror. The means to contend with death has become death.' *White Noise* and *Libra* will explore the American politics of death. Meanwhile Axton's firm continues its connection with the C.I.A. DeLillo prepares for *Libra*:

If America is the world's myth, then the CIA is America's myth. All the themes are there, in tiers of silence, whole bureaucracies of silence, inconspiracies and doublings and brilliant betrayals. . . . It gives a classical tone to our commonly felt emotions.

Two men fire on Axton in the British Columbia woods—from the Autonomous People's Initiative—and he reports all he knows to the Ministry of Public Order. Then he visits the Acropolis with a readiness 'deeper than the art and mathematics embodied in the structure . . . this open cry, this voice we know as our own'. Other visitors speak their languages in the temple which is the example of non-destructive creativity: 'We bring to the temple not prayer or chant or slaughtered rams. Our offering is language.' He is finally reading his son Tap's non-fiction novel in its own 'fresh' language. His son has inherited the father's fascination with language, but creatively.

The sexuality of power, the point where weapons, pornography and organization meet, is the location of *Running Dog* (1978). But the novel also investigates writing after the Civil Rights movement, and the Vietnam and anti-Vietnam behaviour of Americans. What 'the Movement' of the 1960s fought against enters the network processes. Senator Lloyd Percival's wife 'has been reading the Warren Report for eight or nine years . . . Twenty-six volumes. She wears a bed jacket.' Earl Mudger is part of the investigation of Percival's inquiry into certain national corruptions, but he is immediately the voice of DeLillo's subject:

> Loyalties are so interwoven, the thing's a game. The Senator and PAC/ORD aren't nearly the antagonists the public believes them to be. . . . They make deals, they buy people, they sell favours . . . agencies allow this to go on all the time. People know what's happening. But they allow it. You go to bed with your enemies. . . . Sometimes this is so much fun, I'd do it for nothing. . . . We have some Vietnamese here, definitely. . . . Compared to the life most of these people have had, getting out of Saigon was on the level of an escapade . . . Ho Chi Minh City. A lark with firecrackers.

This programme is 'Radial Matrix', 'systems', a network of drug and technology, software and hardware, and electronics: 'Devices make everyone pliant. There's a general sponginess, a lack of conviction. . . . We won far's I'm concerned. Revise the texts.' The '60s' underground information magazine *Running Dog*, briefly cited in an earlier novel, has become an organ of secret connections, 'propaganda mechanism' and 'world wide conspiracy, fantastic assassination schemes'—like the fascination with drugs and devices, a substitute for 'genuine attachments'. Within politics stirs erotics, 'sex as big business', the field of Moll Robbins, journalist on *Running Dog*, Lightbourne's gallery *Cosmic Erotics*, and DeLillo's transient figure, Glen Selvy. Lightbourne tells Moll how he sold a 'highly aroused' Egyptian fertility god ring to an ex-Nazi 'for a pretty sum', and it 'ended up on the finger of King Farouk'—the 'worldwide network', now focussed for DeLillo's plot on 'unedited footage. One copy. The camera original. Shot in Berlin, April, the year 1945 . . . under the Reich Chancellery . . . filmed record of orgy . . . People will kill to obtain it', and especially 'the whole smut-industry power structure'. DeLillo's film—based themes re-surface:

> They put everything on film. . . . Film was essential to the Nazi era. Myth, dreams, memory. . . . If it's Nazis, it's automatically erotic. The violence, the rituals, the leather, the jackboots. The whole thing of uniforms and paraphernalia. He whipped his niece . . . Hitler.

But it also sounds like a description of international brothel culture, the Manson-biker satanists cult interactions, or the military anywhere. Moll, of the ex-'60s 'organ of discontent'—'we say "fuck" all the time'—moves in.

Selvy, to whom 'the quality of transience appealed', lives armed night and day as staff-member of Percival's investigation of Personnel Advisory Committee, Office of Records and Disbursement, 'ostensibly a co-ordinating arm of the whole US intelligence apparatus'. Moll's editor, Grace Delaney, is just as abribed with network; she 'used to spend all her time raising bail for well-hung Panthers', and now, she says, 'I miss conspiracy . . . a sense of evil design.' So now, for *Running Dog*, 'conspiracy's our theme'. In section III–2, Selvy thinks in the characteristic manner of DeLillo's transients in sacrificial networks, headed for an endland:

> He was starting to understand what it all meant. All that test-
> ing. The polygraphs. The rigorous physicals. The semisecrecy.
> All those weeks at the Mines. Electronics. Code-breaking.
> Currencies. Weapons. Survival. . . . The small doses of geo-
> politics. The psychology of terrorism. . . . The double life. His
> private discipline. His hand guns. His regard for precautions,
> how your mind works. The narrowing of choices. . . . All this
> time he'd been preparing to die . . . how to be killed by your
> own side, in secret, no hard feelings. . . . They'd spotted his
> potential, his capacity for favorable development . . . a ritual
> preparation. . . . All conspiracies begin with self-repression.
> They'd seen his potential. . . . The computer approved.

P.A.C./O.R.D. is in fact 'a cover-up for Radial Matrix',
one more 'US Guv' 'centralized finding mechanism for
covert operations directed against foreign governments, and
against political parties trying to gain power contrary to the
interests of US corporations abroad'. Percival grasps its relationship to a main action in the '60s: 'If you study the history
of reform you'll see there's always a counteraction built in.
A low-lying surly passion. Always people ready to invent
new secrets, new bureaucracies of terror.' This is again the
world of Chomsky's book and *Libra,* ten years later (1988):
P.A.C./O.R.D. activities and 'CIA extravagances' 'fill those
small dark places. And they're illegal. Run counter to the
spirit and letter of every law, every intelligence directive, that
pertains to such matters.' The co-ordinator of Radial Matrix is
therefore the man everyone must fear, Mudger, a summary
of DeLillo's late twentieth-century villainy:

> He's got all kinds of links, organized crime and so on. . . . He
> wants to diversify . . . the combination of business drives and
> lusts and impulses with police techniques, with ultrasophisti-
> cated skills of detection, surveillance, extortion, terror and the
> rest of it.

He works on 'confidential information on the accounts of
roughly five hundred taxpayers', obtained from an Inland
Revenue superviser. Needless to say, the Dallas assassination and the Southeast Asia war, the anti-war and civil
rights movements, have to be used as locations where fiction, myth and history suffuse. Mudger is Vietnam-trained;

Radial Matrix uses 'an assassination team of former ARVN rangers'—'evidence that adjustment had to be made.' And it is here that the languages of systems controls reappear in familiar form:

> Vietnam, in more ways than one, was a war based on hybrid gibberish. But Mudger could understand the importance of this on the most basic level, where the fighting man stood and where technical idiom was often the only element of precision, the only true beauty, he could take with him into realms of ambiguity. . . . Spoken about by sweaty men in camouflage grease, these number-words and coinages had the inviolate grace of a strict metre of chant. . . . Reciting these names was the soldier's poetry, his counterjargon to death.

Domestically, the death to be countered is systematic surveillance and espionage:

> When technology reaches a certain level, people begin to feel like criminals. Someone is after you, the computer maybe, the machine-police. You can't escape investigation. The facts about you and your whole existence have been collected or are being collected. Banks, insurance companies, credit organizations, tax examiners, passport offices, reporting services, police agencies, intelligence gatherers. . . . If *they* issue a print-out saying we're guilty, then we're guilty. But it goes even deeper, doesn't it? It's the presence alone, the very fact, the superabundance of technology, that makes us feel we're committing crimes. . . . What complex programmes. And there's no one to explain it to us.

By extension, gun infatuation is surveillance: 'The weapon was firing *him*. . . . Right, that's right, a regular jerk off. . . . The feeling in this outfit concerning devices of any kind is close to religious.' Selvy's ambiguous release (in Part III, Section 3) is a kind of endland, therefore:

> All behind him now. Cities, buildings, people, systems. All the relationships and links. The plan, the execution, the sequel. . . . All that coherence. Selection, election, option, alternative. All behind him now. Codes and formats. Courses of action. Values, bias, predilection.
> Choice is a subtle form of disease.

Once again, DeLillo draws his transient towards non-violent,

Asian quietism. Selvy takes lessons in meditation from Levi Blackwater, ex-technical adviser to the A.R.V.N., tortured by the Vietcong and surviving into a death of the self within 'spiritual unity'. These episodes are simultaneous with a showing of the actual bunker film—mainly Hitler's startling mimic ability. Levi gives Selvy a kind of Indian burial—'on a wooden framework of rudimentary platform', chanting to direct 'the separation of the deceased from his body, as taught by the masters of the snowy range. This was a *lama* function.' Selvy's end zone island is a traditionally non-destructive religious release from enclosing systems. The bunker film exposes a comedy of pathos edged with violence, the ridiculousness of both power and powerlessness. And the ridiculousness of Nazism is transferred, in *White Noise* (1985), to Jack Gladney's School of Hitler Studies, part of a system of university courses on popular arts, car crashes, cereal box texts (a jab at Barthes), and so forth. Hitler studies reduces European crisis to classroom interests and entertainments, taught by fashionable, apparently authentic academics—'smart, thuggish, movie-mad, trivia-crazed . . . here to decipher the natural language of the culture, to make a formal method of the shiny pleasures they'd known in their Europe-shadowed childhoods.' Over their need for cult and interpretation powers hovers an actuality—the double; parody of DeLillo's narrative: 'The enormous dark mass moved like some death ship in a Norse legend, escorted across the night by armoured creatures with spiral wings.' Industrial strikes again, in mythicized absurdity.

The Gladney family parodies American divorce families—half brothers and sisters, step-children, former wife with the C.I.A., and another in an ashram system as Mother Devi—a system of survival in miniature, now threatened by the cloud. Once again, there is an expert to language it away: 'This is Nyodene D. A whole new generation of toxic waste.' In parallel, Gladney is hunting for Dylar, an experimental drug that cures fear of death—appropriate because this is a society that threatens itself. The 'white noise' of the title is, after all, a lethal version of the ubiquitous noise that electronically and mechanically invades human life in the late twentieth century, taken by millions to be a continuous need, a man-made curse, and there is no god or devil to blame. As William Burroughs defined addiction in 1959: 'The face of "evil" is always the face of total need.' America, DeLillo's death system in this novel, is a network of controls and needs for which no one will or can accept responsibility. Every person consumes the culture and receives its electronic stimuli. Objects therefore have 'darkness attached to them, a foreboding'. Children are vulnerable, so Gladney names his son Heinrich, hoping to 'shield him, make him unafraid', name him so that 'an authority might cling to him'. But Heinrich organizes his own system—exchanges chess moves with an imprisoned murderer, lives in introspective uncertainty, in a biological determinism which reflects back to the designs in *Ratner's Star*: 'all this activity of the brain and you don't know what's you and what's some neuron that just happen to fire. . . . Isn't that just why Tommy Ray killed those people?' In fact, the children alert parents to the social conditions, as well as being a major resource for media and advertising networks, a whiteness of noise controls. In a comment for the *New York Times Book Review*, to accompany a review of *White Noise*,[13] DeLillo stated that the book's children

> are a form of magic. The adults are mystified by all the data that flows through their lives, but the children carry the data and absorb it most deeply. They give family life a buzz and hum; it's almost another form of white noise.

Once they are students—at least at this university—they are informed they will never participate in the making of America: 'It is only a matter of time before you experience the vast loneliness and dissatisfaction of consumers who have lost their group identity.' Gladney enters further into DeLillo's analysis of American revisions of fascism and religious obsession: 'Crowds came to hear Hitler speak, crowds erotically charged, masses he once called his only bride. . . . Crowds came to form a shield . . . to become a crowd is to keep out death.' The literature of 'crowds and power' is extensive. DeLillo's contribution is to recognize, as Goebbels did, that popular culture can be used as state control through electronic media. Naturally, it is a former

New York sports writer, Murray J. Siskind, who controls 'American environment' studies—in the same building as Gladney's Hitler studies: 'He is now your Hitler. . . . It was masterful, shrewd and stunningly preemptive. It's what I want to do with Elvis.' These academics need to be sole controllers of data systems, masters of white noise, that 'remote and steady murmur around our sleep, as of dead souls babbling at the edge of a dream'. Television is studied as

> the primal force in the American home, sealed-off, self-contained, self-referring . . . a wealth of data concealed in the grids, in the bright packaging, the jingles, the slice-of-life commercials, the products hurtling out of darkness, the coded messages . . . like chants. . . . Coke is it. Coke is it. Coke is it . . . sacred formulas . . . mechanism of offering a hopeful twist to apocalyptic events.

Television is the network of need become the death design of a culture. In the *New York Times* interview, DeLillo stated:

> Maybe the fact that death permeates the book made me retreat into comedy. . . . I never set out to write an apocalyptic novel. It's about death on the individual level. Only Hitler is large enough and terrible enough to absorb and neutralize Jack Gladney's obsessive fears of dying. . . . Jack uses Hitler as a protective device; he wants to grasp anything he can. . . . [For Murray J. Siskind the supermarket is] rich in magic and dread. Perhaps the supermarket tabloids are the richest materials of all, closest to the spirit of the book. They ask profoundly important questions about death, the after-life, God, worlds and space, yet they exist in an almost Pop Art atmosphere.

It is here that white noise is supreme; language code dominates; and Asian method is remote:

> The toneless system, the jangle and skid of carts, the loudspeakers and the coffee-making machines, the cries of children. And over it all . . . the dull and unbreakable roar, as of some form of swarming life just outside the range of human apprehension. . . . Everything is concealed in symbolism. . . . The large doors slide open, they close unbidden. Energy waves, incident radiation . . . code words and ceremonial phrases. It is just a question of deciphering. . . . Not that we

> would want to. . . . This is not Tibet . . . Tibetans try to see
> death for what it is. It is the end of attachment to things. . . .
> But once we stop denying death, we can proceed calmly to
> die. . . . We simply walk toward the sliding doors. . . . Look
> how well-lighted everything is . . . sealed off . . . timeless.
> Another reason why I think of Tibet. Dying is an art in
> Tibet. . . . Chants, numerology, horoscopes, recitations. Here
> we don't die, we shop. But the difference is less marked than
> you think.

But Gladney is right the first time. The difference from Tibet
is massive. University, supermarket and toxic waste disasters
are parts of the deathly network, sacrificial, suicidal, Americana. The families are evacuated but the military use the
event 'in order to rehearse the simulation' called Simuvac.
After exposure to Nyodene D, Gladney becomes an interesting subject: 'I tapped into your history. I'm getting bracketed
numbers with pulsing stars'—'Am I going to die?'—'Not in
so many words'—'How many words does it take?'—'it's
not a question of words. It's a question of years. We'll
know in fifteen years. In the meantime we definitely have a
situation. . . . I wouldn't worry . . . I'd go ahead and save
my life . . .'—'But you said we have a situation'—'I didn't
say it. The computer did.' Heinrich is correct: 'What good is
knowledge if it just floats in the air? It goes from computer
to computer. . . . But nobody actually knows anything.'
The local hospital nuns confess: 'As belief shrinks from the
world, people find it more necessary than ever that *someone*
believe. . . . Nuns in black. . . . We surrender ourselves to
make your nonbelief possible. . . . There is no truth without
fools.'
Truth is a word whose meaning has to be continually
decoded. Everything appears to signify what those in control need and invent, and the rest believe. *White Noise* may
be read as a black farce on Foucault's idea of suicidally
destructive information, as a sardonic assault on semio-
tics as a destructive science of signs. Analysis has reached
a dead end. The rest is David Cronenberg's *Videodrome*.
Drugs are essential survival devices, whether they work
or not. Meanwhile 'air currents that carry industrial waste'
degenerate everything in their course: 'Man's guilt in history

and in the tides of his own blood has been complicated by technology, the daily seeping falsehearted death.' In Chapter 21, Gladney's wife reads out a front-page story: 'Life After Death Guaranteed with Bonus Coupons'—it concerns Princeton's Institute for Advanced Studies discovering 'absolute and undeniable proof of life after death', through patients under hypno-regression. The story is a black, hilarious spoof of immortality needs. Gladney's first-person narrative concludes:

> This is the whole point of technology. It creates an appetite for immortality on the one hand. It threatens universal extinction on the other. Technology is removed from nature. . . . Hopeless and fearful people are drawn to magical figures mythic figures, epic men who intimidate and darkly loom.

His Hitler studies exemplify that need, and DeLillo's *Libra* (1988) takes on the appalling Americana dominance of the most recent epic myth of dominance by epic network and its dark figures.

The C.I.A. 'darkly looms' frequently in the novels, together with the rest of the networks of control across the world. 'History as fiction, fiction as history'—the maxim generates the non-fiction novel and Norman Mailer's novel as history, history as the novel in *The Armies of the Night* (1968) and other works of the 1960s. The Kennedy assassination of 22 November 1963, on television, and Lee Harvey Oswald's murder, on television, forty-eight hours later, now constitute a quarter of a century of data, interpretation and myth. DeLillo needs to append a note to *Libra*—that this is a fiction about 'a major unresolved event', whose characters are 'altered and embellished', and that his contribution 'is one more gloom in the chronicle of unknowing', 'speculation that widens with the years'. This huge novel emerges from the multiple interface of many previous texts, including official reports on the event, but also a proliferation of exposures of C.I.A. activities throughout the world, texts which continue to appear and about which little or nothing is officially done.[14] In 1964, the Warren Report, so much consumed by Senator Percival's wife in *Running Dog*, concluded that Oswald shot Kennedy, acting alone. Fifteen years later, the House Select Committee on Assassination decided he was most probably part of a conspiracy. In fact, conspiracy theories, implicating systems from the Mafia to the C.I.A., have spawned continuously. In 1986 appeared a five-and-a-half-hour T.V. trial of Oswald, partly acted by a judge and some lawyers—one of them prosecuted Charles Manson, another defended Karen Silk, and the jury were Dallas citizens. *Libra* uses established incidents, characters and facts, and invents others, and assembles these data into an interpretation. The fervour of its energies includes, and in fact is in many ways based on, the kind of indictment I. F. Stone stated on 9 December 1963 in his *Weekly*,[15] pointing to national involvement of the kind DeLillo uses in *White Noise*:

> Have we not become conditioned to the notion that we should have a secret agency of government—the CIA—with secret funds, to wield the dagger beneath the cloak against leaders we dislike? . . . In this sense we share the guilt with Oswald and Ruby and rightist crackpots. Where the right to kill is so universally accepted, we should not be surprised if our young President was slain. It is not just the ease in obtaining guns, it is the ease in obtaining excuses, that fosters assassination. This is more urgently in need of examination than those who pulled the trigger. . . . The Kennedy Administration, in violation of our own laws and international law, permitted that invasion from our shores which ended so ingloriously in the Bay of Pigs. . . . it would be well to think it over carefully before canonizing Kennedy as an apostle of peace.

Libra is part of that needed 'examination', part of the investigation of what Stone had earlier called (26 April 1961) America's process of 'self-destruction': The chain reaction is already in motion. . . . We cannot set up government agencies empowered to act lawlessly without infecting the life of our own Republic.'

This essay is not the place to examine DeLillo's interpretation of the data. Nor will it follow through the obvious relationships of the novel to the concerns and characters of the previous novels. Any consistent reader will find that clear for himself, and indeed this essay has hopefully done a good deal of the work. Suffice it to point out one or two landmarks in the immense location of the narrative. Oswald is clearly the most recent of DeLillo's transients who reach an end zone of murder and victimization, within global intersections. The novel opens, in fact, with a letter from him to his brother that begins the fatal projection of his career: 'Happiness is taking part in the struggle, where there is no borderline between one's personal world, and the world in general.' Permissive innocence begins here, and the self-referential career as Marine, Soviet citizen, defector, and employee of the C.I.A. and F.B.I. DeLillo dramatizes both his and the C.I.A. agents' need not just to affect 'history', but to *feel* they do. At the very first link between them, Captain Ferrie tells Oswald, in familiar terms:

> I've studied patterns of coincidence. How patterns emerge outside the bounds of cause and effect. I've studied geopolitics at Baldwin-Wallace before it was called geopolitics. . . . I'm constantly haunted by the thought of cops, government cops, Feebies—the FBI. . . . Once you get into the files, they never leave you alone. They stick to you like cancer. Eternal.

And later: 'I'm the dark scary side of John Glenn. Great health except for the cancer eating my brain.' As a key metonymy for social disease, cancer is already familiar from the fiction of Henry Miller and Norman Mailer, and from the psychoanalytical texts of Wilhelm Reich. Oswald begins his training as victim at an early age with dreams of himself as hero of secret actions—'reverie of control, perfection of rage, perfection of desire'—and he fits the Agency need, expressed by Win Everett, as he devises its assassin: 'a general shape, a life. . . . They wanted a name, a face, a bodily frame they might use to extend their fiction into the world.' Oswald begins to be their 'script'.

At the enclosed centre of *Libra* sits a new figure in DeLillo's fictions, Nicholas Branch at the C.I.A.'s Historical Intelligence Collection. His job is to handle the continually appearing masses of data on the presidential assassination, 'names of witnesses, informers, investigators, people linked to Lee H. Oswald, people linked to Jack Ruby, all conveniently suggestively dead. . . . conspiracy, coincidence, loose ends, dead ends, multiple interpretations'. No need, he thinks, 'to

invent the grand and masterful scheme, the plot that reaches
flawlessly in a dozen directions. Still, the cases do resonate,
don't they?' Branch is DeLillo's data-assembler trapped in
the network as its scribe, as DeLillo's *alter scriptor*, absorbed
in 'a vast and rhythmic coincidence, a daisy chain of rumour,
suspicion and secret wish'. Branch has 'abandoned his life
to understanding that moment in Dallas'. He even believes
the Warren Report is 'the megaton novel James Joyce would
have written if he'd moved to Iowa City and lived to be
a hundred'. But Joyce's two epics of 'the seim anew' are
created works of art, not propaganda or nonfiction novels of
psychological and political corruption. Branch further reads
the Report as 'a ruined city of trivia where people feel real
pain. This is the Joycean Book of America, remember—the
novel in which nothing is left out.' But, again, neither a novel
nor a report can be total, and in any case 'data never ceases
to accumulate and need continual assemblage. . . . Powerful
events breed their own network of inconsistencies. The
simple facts elude authentication.' A 'coherent history' will
always be a 'premature' notion: 'data keeps coming . . . new
lives enter the record all the time. The past is changing as he
writes.' But since it is too extensive to know, it thrills because
it is cosmic. Branch is as excited as Bannister, ex-F.B.I. man
working for the C.I.A., except that the latter is essentially
extra-legal:

> We have this dilemma we have to face. Serious men deprived
> of an outlet. . . . Everyday lawful pursuits don't meet our
> special requirements . . . a special society that pretty much
> satisfied the most serious things in my nature. Secrets to trade
> and keep, certain dangers, an opportunity to function in tight
> spots, wave a gun in people's faces. That's a charmed society.
> If you've got criminal tendencies . . . one of the places to make
> your mark is law enforcement. . . . We invent a society where
> it's always wartime. The law has little to give.

DeLillo knows that desire to control is always manic
and thrusts towards fulfilment in the extra-legal. The Cuban
rebels' trainer, Mackey, understands this: the CIA 'was set
up to obscure the deeper responsibilities, the calls of blood
trust that have to be answered . . . men stranded in the
smoke of remote meditations.' And it is religious—Win

Everett again: 'Like ancient monks . . . these systems collect and process. All the secret knowledge of the world.' Life is cult 'fantasies', a religion based on coincidences and warfare. Oswald is attracted to Soviet Communism as the C.I.A. man is to the Agency: 'a special language', 'a secret level where those outside the cadre could not gain access to it' and know 'the true names of operations'. And 'there was a natural kinship between business and intelligence work'. Cuban invasion is especially dear to the C.I.A. for its investments there—'enormous personal gain' beyond 'legitimate profits'. One member, Parmenter, says he 'could not always tell where the Agency left off and the corporations began'. Cuba equals 'unexplored oil properties'. The language issues are also familiar: 'this gibberish had the sound of a mind unravelling.'

Everett's pleasure in his Oswald script is explicit: 'Stalking a victim can be a way of organizing one's loneliness, making a network out of it, a fabric of connections. Desperate men give their solitude a purpose and a destiny.' Oswald in the U.S.S.R. enables DeLillo to parallel the C.I.A. with the K.G.B., and then he extends them both to parallel 'the Carmine Latta network rackets of Cuban dope, Central American dope, casinos and betting parlours'. For Latta, Bobby Kennedy is the focus of 'a determined rage, but fine and precise, carefully formed', and this is the system into which Jack Ruby moves towards his assassination of Oswald: Florida's 'biggest industry' and its links to pre-Castro Cuba ('fucking paradise then'). So the Agency and Latta are drawn together when the President 'put out the word he wanted Castro dead'. These people are essentially stateless and transient. Oswald needs their system against loneliness and 'incompleteness', and so does Ruby. They both become victims of the new desire of the C.I.A.: not 'the once bold idea of assassinating Castro . . . the man we really want is JFK . . . a surgical miss'. Ironically, Oswald wants to kill Governor Connally, since, among other things, he feels let down by the Marines (he believes Connally is secretary of the Navy). But, as Everett, in many ways DeLillo's voice on plots—they 'carry their own logic' and tend 'to move toward death'—the rest of the passage is used at the opening of

94

this essay. The irony of Ruby is his sentimental patriotism and his pride in being 'a friend of the police in the most pro-American city anywhere in the world'. He fits into the Dallas Americana majority who panic into belief that the Real Control Apparatus is always in charge:

> The Christian Crusade women, the John Birchmen, the semi-retired, the wrathful, the betrayed, the ones who keep coming up empty. . . . The Apparatus paralyzed not only our armed forces but our individual lives, frustrating every normal American ambition, infiltrating our minds and bodies with fluoridation, with the creeping fever of trade unions and the left-wing press and the income tax, every modern sickness that saps the nation's will to resist the enemy advance. The Red Chinese are massing below the California border. There are confirmed reports. . . . The Apparatus is precisely what we can't see or name. . . . It is the mystery we can't get hold of, the plot that we can't uncover.

The novel's title is derived from an equally powerful plot in the universe—astrology. A bogus occultist tells Oswald he is a Libran—in fact, a negative Libran, unsteadily and impulsively balanced, 'poised to make a dangerous leap'.

As they move towards Dallas, Kennedy says to Jacqueline: 'we're headed into nut country now', and indeed the city is packed with Americans in need of magic leadership—'here to surround the brittle body of one man and claim his smile, receive some token of the bounty of his soul'. The network monad gradually completes. The 'surgical miss' failed, and the C.I.A. always fears accidents. Oswald must be sacrificed so that the Agencies survive—and, of course, they are a mythical actuality financed by the American citizens as part of their Americana needs. But larger questions hover in the sinister atmosphere. Are Tap's nonfiction novel, Brademas's dig, and the Tibetan relinquishments of self and objects all that may be rescued from overwhelmingly entropic needs for murder and suicide, for network thrills and destructive creativity? Is the permanent circumstance only what Anthony Wilden suggests for this society's epistemology—a kind of ' "security operation" of madness' in an intolerable environment? What form of revolt—'inside and against'—could possibly modify 'US Guv' and its systems? DeLillo's fictions indicate that there are real human needs for this epistemology. Their massive data assemblages tend to overwhelm their frequently satirical approaches:

> The means of analysis—metalanguage—like the observer, is also part of the system being analyzed. In a word, we must always and inevitably face paradoxes—both existential and logical—which cannot in any circumstances be resolved.

Information in control structures is negative entropy 'because it maintains, reproduces, and increases organization', and language

> is not only a means of communication and behaviour; it also imposes specific systemic and structural constraints on the ways in which we perceived and act upon the world and each other. . . . The metasystem can profitably be described as an overdetermined set of propositions in a metalanguage.

But, as DeLillo shows, networks are 'forms of pathological communication' that 'convert themselves into power relationships'.[16] He is the senior novelist of these conditions and their needs, far beyond their local locations. As Prigogine and Stengers state it in their postface to Michel Serres's *Hermes*: 'The passage from local to global' is an obsessional need, and not at all only for mathematicians and physicists, but for the majority of human beings, either throughout their lives or at certain occasions of crisis or happiness. 'The question of the integrable world authorizes dreams of determinism' which fuse into the 'dream of omniscience', a dangerous form of Leibnizian monadology. DeLillo expertly explores the dynamics of this passage, proposing that epic coherences are fiction in one sense but also real needs of irrational human requirement for meaning, for a 'language of dynamics', for a 'Lebnizian system of the world in which every point locally expresses the global law'. In Serres's terms, 'the monad automatically deciphers, both in itself and for itself, a universe that is at once its closed interior [and] its own account of it.' DeLillo represents the kinetics of the control desire for 'integrable system', and as Prigogine and Stengers observe 'our formalized science' today is 'a world in which interactions play an ever more important rôle'.[17] The needs for a Grand Theory and for its agents and practitioners remains. DeLillo's novels poise a reader between appreciation and destructive criticism of those needs and their dire consequences.

NOTES

1. DeLillo's novels were first published in the United States in the following editions: *Americana* (Boston: Houghton Mifflin, 1971); *Great Jones Street* (Boston: Houghton Mifflin, 1973); *End Zone* (New York: Pocket Books, 1973); *Ratner's Star* (New York: Knopf, 1976); *Players* (New York: Knopf, 1977); *Running Dog* (New York: Knopf, 1978); *The Names (New York: Vintage Books, 1983); White Noise* (New York: Viking, 1985); and *Libra* (New York: Viking, 1988).
2. Erich Heller, *The Disinherited Mind* excerpted in; ed. Ronald Gray, *Kafka* (New Jersey: Prentice Hall, 1962), p. 115.
3. Jacques Ellul, *Propaganda: The Formation of Men's Attitudes* (1962; New York: Knopf, 1965), pp. 121–22, x–xi, 3, 175, 254.
4. Lionel Abel, *Metatheatre: A New View of Dramatic Form* (New York: Hill and Wang, 1963).
5. Christian K. Messenger, *Sport and the Spirit of Play in American Fiction*, (New York: Columbia University Press, 1981), pp. xi, 1, 3, 8.
6. Georges Bataille, *Visions of Excess: Selected Writings 1927–1939*, ed. Alan Stoekl (Manchester University Press, 1985).
7. Jacques Attali, *Noise: The Political Economy of Music* (1977; Manchester: Manchester University Press, 1985), pp. 3–5, 8, 110–11.
8. 'Paranoia' according to *The Shorter Oxford English Dictionary*: 'Path. Mental derangement; *spec.* chronic mental unsoundness characterized by delusions and hallucinations.'
9. Gershon G. Scholem, *On the Kabbalah and its Symbolism* (New York: Schocken Books, 1969), pp. 35, 73, 102.
10. Noam Chomsky, *The Culture of Terrorism* (London: Pluto Press, 1988), p. 2.
11. Scott Fitzgerald, *Tender is the Night* (1934), Bk. 5, Ch. 12; Edmund Wilson (ed.), *The Crack-Up* (New York: New Directions, 1965), pp. 60–70.
12. Paul Feyerabend, *Farewell to Reason* (London: Verso, 1987); Rupert Sheldrake, *The Presence of the Past* (London: Collins, 1988).
13. Coryn James, 'I Never Set Out to Write an Apocalyptic Novel', *New York Times Book Review*, 3 November 1985, p. 30.

14. For example, the report on *Drugs, Law Enforcement and Foreign Policy* issued by the Senate Committee on Narcotics, 13 April 1989, reports on C.I.A. operations in El Salvador since 1977, etc. . . .
15. I. F. Stone, *In Time of Torment* (New York: Vintage Books, 1968), pp. 8, 14.
16. Anthony Wilden, *System and Structure: Essays in Communication and Exchange* (London: Tavistock Publications, 1972), pp. 206, 94, 203, 210.
17. Ilya Prigogine and Isabelle Stengers, 'Postface: Dynamics from Leibniz to Lucretius' in J. V. Harari and D. F. Bell (eds.), *Michel Serres – Hermes: Literature, Science, Philosophy* (Baltimore and London: Johns Hopkins, 1982), pp. 138, 142.

4

Investing the Glimpse: Raymond Carver and the Syntax of Silence

BY GRAHAM CLARKE

1

Raymond Carver's death from cancer in August 1988 brought to a close the career of a writing talent which had established itself as one of the leading voices in what might be seen as a larger renaissance of the American short story. Born in 1939 at Clatskanie, Oregon, Carver's life offers an American success story the very opposite of the lives he depicts in his fiction. As Michael Foley notes,

> Raymond Carver is a typically American hero, a kind of literary Rocky—janitor, delivery man, sawmill operator, service-station attendant, an uneducated alcoholic no-hoper who rises to Major Writer status and the Professorship of English at Syracuse University.[1]

Carver's fiction, however, remains wedded to the world he knew before academia: a transient blue-collar middle America which exists in a twilight zone devoid of the 'hyper-reality' constructed in the media's myths of a consumer America. Carver's characters move between the 'margins of middle-class life' and the 'brink of lumpen existence'.[2] If alcohol features so prominently in this world, as it did in Carver's own life, it is because it is part of a numbing process whereby the very emptiness his stories depict is kept at bay. These are people who 'got lost' in their lives 'same as I got lost in mine'. People who live in an America which, far from the symbolic daylight of California, has 'gone from afternoon to night'. It is also invariably a world of silence, of vacuum, and of absence: a world in which the stories seek not so much to resolve the terms of the lives depicted, as to sense the implications of that silence and absence. To bring to the reader, in other words, the measure of those lives as they are felt. As such Carver remains his own most typical character and his life the definitive story, for 'as Hemingway correctly pointed out, all stories, if continued far enough, end in death. Truly.'

Carver's early death in itself suggests something of the very ambience of his fiction and makes clear how pervasive the continuing fear and anxiety of death (and cancer) is to the lives he depicts. Carver's characters live lives of 'pain and humiliation', ostensibly failed lives in which divorce, unemployment, boredom, and paranoia exist as part of an everyday landscape: the inversion of the American dream. The suburbs in which they seek resolution (or simply a way to get through their day) consist of vacant habitats where death exists as a kind of continuing reminder of personal limits. Death frames Carver's world and suggests an underlying nothingness: the existential terms of an American *sans* its transcendent possibilities. The overall mood is that of an America as a single, but empty and dark, shopping mall. Indeed, in a story central to the *oeuvre* (and to which I shall return) Carver distinguishes his writing from any belief in affairs of the spirit. In 'Errand' (1988), a story about the death of Chekhov, Carver sides with the playwright (and short story writer) against the philosophy of Tolstoy. Chekhov is in hospital when Tolstoy visits him:

> He had to listen, amazedly, as the count began to discourse on his theories of the immortality of the soul. Concerning that visit, Chekhov later wrote, 'Tolstoy assumes that all of us . . . live on in a principle (such as reason or love) the essence of which are a mystery to us. . . . I have no use for that kind of immortality.'[3]

This could be Carver speaking, just as later in the story he again quotes Chekhov approvingly in a similar critique of Tolstoyan philosophy: 'And as far as his outlook on life and writing went,' Carver writes,

> he once told someone that he lacked 'a political, religious, and philosophical world view. I change it every month, so I'll have to limit myself to the description of how my heroes love, marry, give birth, die, and how they speak.'

That, in other words, which can be apprehended 'by one or more of [the] five senses'.[4]

That knowledge which can be 'apprehended' by the senses underlies Carver's ambivalent search for meaning in a world which resists interpretation. Indeed, significantly it is a basic aspect of his attempt to 'know' his father, as he makes clear in a semi-autobiographical piece entitled 'My Father's Life': a 'sketch' whose attempts at some kind of final knowledge end only in the overwhelming admission of the certainties of death and absence. As such the account is central to the Carver effect, pointing up, in a personal and private context, the ethos which, at the end of his publishing career, he gives to Chekhov. Just as he shares his father's name (Clevie Raymond Carver and Raymond Clevie Carver, Jr., although his mother called his father Raymond) so his father's death suggests the very terms on which Carver approaches life. For Carver's sense of his father, as both a personality and a person, is defined through absence. He seeks an identity which cannot be gauged, much less touched. His father, like his name and life, remains an enigma. All that Carver can do is to take succour from personal artifacts as the evidence of what was. Significantly he turns to a photograph of his father as a young man; and yet the photograph compounds the sense of absence and strangeness. His father is there, but is not. No matter how much Carver stares at the photograph he is always left with the fact of its otherness; his father exists as a flat image, a token which seemingly promises everything and yet yields nothing. The glimpse, to Carver, says it all, for all he can do is to look:

> Among the pictures my mother kept of my dad and herself during those early days in Washington was a photograph of

101

him standing in front of a car, holding a beer and a stringer of fish. In the photograph he is wearing his hat back on his forehead and has this awkward grin on his face. I asked her for it and she gave it to me, along with some others. I put it up on my wall, and each time we moved, I took the picture along and put it up on another wall. I looked at it carefully from time to time, trying to figure out some things about my dad, and maybe myself in the process. But I couldn't. My dad just kept moving further and further away from me and back into time. Finally, in the course of another move, I lost the photograph.[5]

Later Carver attempts to write a poem about the photograph. Entitled 'Photograph of My Father in His Twenty Second Year' it is offered as 'an attempt to say something about my dad'. The poem is as much a story and has about its title a flatness redolent of Carver's viewpoint. It suggests the way Carver approaches the materials of his fiction, for the photograph defines the terms on which the subject, and a life, can be viewed. Carver looks at the image, endlessly probing its details in order to establish a definitive sense of the subject but all he sees is an image of an individual at once unknowable and ungraspable. The photograph encapsulates a condition which it refuses to reveal. It announces absence by its very presence. It freezes an entire history in a syntax of silence. Carver can only look and perhaps glimpse what lies beneath the surface and frame around the figure as he seeks what Barthes calls a 'punctum'—a point of contact through which meaning suddenly erupts. For Carver there is only an overwhelming absence. The palpable insists on the impalpable. All that remains is the look of a son at an image of his dead father: a silent but inevitable admission of loss and, by implication, pain.

And this, of course, is Carver's point: for the photograph reflects not just one history, but a series of histories all of which are lost and yet all of which set the terms of Carver's own life. But how are those 'histories' to be known? In part, perhaps, Carver's response is suggested by the fact that 'My Father's Life' is only some eight-and-a-half pages long. In a culture where autobiography and biography are acknowledged as major genres, Carver not only reduces the terms of his father's life, he gives to the account a quietism which borders on silence. There can be no celebration. All that we have is a condition, which through the sparely given details, achieves an extraordinary complexity and resonance. Once again, the detail, so to speak, like the moment, becomes the punctum of meaning. As Frank Kermode has said, Carver's is a 'fiction so spare in manner that it takes time before one realizes how completely a whole culture and a whole moral condition are being represented by even the most seemingly slight sketch',[6] or, in this instance, a photograph.

And it is, indeed, this sense of spareness and marvellous economy which so underlines his relationship to the American short story, for the nub of Carver's fiction is its intensity. He is content to observe his subjects in a frozen moment of time and yet brings to bear on that moment the entire weight of their histories and life. Like the photograph of his father, his stories mine silence and otherness. They achieve a texture of nuance and shadow in which less is invariably more. A syntax of silence makes the glimpse the primary act of knowing and, ultimately, communication. As Carver says in a poem called, significantly, 'Reading' (for this is what looking is), 'Every man's life is a mystery, even as/ yours is, and mine'[7] and, of course, his father's.

2

Carver's status as a short story writer has been very much bound up with the 'minimalist' and 'maximalist' debate. And although Carver declared, 'who cares finally what they want to call the stories we write', he remains the quintessential minimalist, seemingly reducing to an absolute spareness both his subject-matter and his treatment of it. Thus the distinction between Tolstoy and Chekhov, and thus equally the penchant for the short story against the novel, for although Carver published poetry (*In a Marine Light*, published in 1988, is the most substantial volume), it is as a writer of stories for which he is most known. Three volumes in particular, *Will you Please be Quiet, Please?* (1976), *What we Talk About When we Talk About Love* (1981), and *Cathedral*

(1983)—all of which were published by Picador as *The Stories of Raymond Carver* (1985) are, together with *Elephant* (1988), the major achievement. It is these that have made him not only a central figure within a revival of the genre but have equally made him a personality at the head of what *Granta* termed 'dirty realism': a fiction concerned primarily with the 'under-belly' of American life.

Certainly Carver saw his commitment to the short story as part of a larger revival of a genre basic to the American tradition, and one wholly appropriate to the fragmented and disparate America of post-Vietnam and Watergate. As Carver noted, 'The current profusion in the writing and publishing of short stories' had not only 'provided the tired blood of mainstream American letters with something new to think about', it had also 'done nothing less than revitalize the national literature'.[8] Large claims indeed.

For the American writer the short story has invariably offered itself as appropriate to a modern condition; as Poe's stories show, as does the writing of two major precursors (and influences) of Carver's, Ernest Hemingway and Sherwood Anderson. Indeed Carver quotes with approval Anderson's belief that 'A man has to begin over and over— to try to think and feel only in a very limited field, the house on the street, the man at the corner drug store.'[9] But Carver does not merely replace the grotesques in *Winesburg, Ohio* (1919) with their contemporary equivalents. His affinity lies in a particular intensity of awareness, which in its democratic commitment to the everyday sees it as part of an endlessly enigmatic dimension of existence. In this sense Carver's subjects—waitresses, postmen, the unemployed, divorced couples, and teachers, for example—whilst familiar as part of an 'everyday' world, are never made ordinary. They exist, pre-eminently as unique entities: photographic images which reflect the individual space of their personal environments. Thus Carver never deals in communities, like Anderson, nor in 'individuals', like Hemingway, nor does he 'celebrate' a moment of assumed contact with an 'ordinary' America like William Carlos Williams. Carver's is a self-consciously limited area of attention in order to achieve as particular a realization as possible of individual marks and spaces; he seeks the terms of individual existences and histories whilst allowing the subjects to retain their meaning and otherness. The deceptive simplicity of style and often restrained and flat tones are part of a larger insistence on an absolute precision of attention: of the eye registering the minutest of details in order to sense the terms of another's existence. As Carver states in 'On Writing':

> It's possible, in a poem or a short story, to write about commonplace things and objects using commonplace but precise language, and to endow those things—a chair, a window curtain, a fork, a stone, a woman's earring—with immense, even startling power. It is possible to write a line of seemingly innocuous dialogue and have it send a chill along the reader's spine—the source of artistic delight, as Nabokov would have it. That's the kind of writing that most interests me.[10]

This is the 'care' which underlies what Carver terms the writer's 'signature' on a subject. The minimalism, as such, is based on an absolute concern with the implications of a single mood: a space of habitation (and consciousness) where the syntax is as much concerned with the silent as it is with the spoken. Once again a moment where the 'other' is glimpsed at a point of possible recognition and knowing:

> The short story writer's task is to invest the glimpse with all that is in his power. He'll bring his intelligence and literary skill to bear (his talent), his sense of proportion and sense of the fitness of things: of how things out there really are and how he sees those things—like no one else sees them.[11]

The act of looking is made central. Indeed, Carver's America is very much a world of people looking *at* one another: through windows, door frames, across rooms and tables; always fixed in a wholly separate and distanced personal space and otherness. They exist amidst a society which surrounds them with a constant stream of images reflecting imagined lives and the myths of an idealized American materialism. We glimpse them caught within this culture of collages; a momentary realization of their histories as wholly displaced from the fictions of the culture in which they exist.

Thus, once again, why the short story is so basic to Carver's reading of contemporary America:

> To write a novel, it seemed to me, a writer should be living in a world that makes sense, a world that the writer can believe in, draw a bead on, and then write about accurately. A world that will, for a time anyway, stay fixed in one place. Along with this there has to be a belief in the essential *correctness* of that world. A belief that the known world has reasons for existing, and is worth writing about, is not likely to go up in smoke in the process. This wasn't the case with the world I knew and was living in. My world was one that seemed to change gears and directions, along with its rules, every day. Time and again I reached the point where I couldn't see or plan any further ahead than the first of next month and gathering together enough money, by hook or by crook, to meet the rent and provide the children's school clothes. This is true.[12]

Like much of Carver's fiction this has a deceptively simple tone to it. The downbeat voice and the pointed dénouement, which reduces his task as a writer to the most basic of aspects, deliberately undercuts the perspectives we have come to associate with the main chance of the American novel. Carver speaks to an America devoid of its unifying myths. It is a world in which the terms of meaning (as of reading) have been displaced by a scattered and fragmented plurality. The short story, as such, offers a 'momentary stay' against the chaos of a public America; an unknowable condition in which individual lives can find no larger perspective other than the terms of their everyday rhythms or the fictions and myths of the culture as reflected through adverts and T.V. The personal here is not so much a retreat as the only space left. As one character says in 'Sixty Acres', 'There was never a place to go'. In Carver's America there *is* nowhere to go. The culture has reached the limits of its own exhaustion. The entropic state so imaged in Pynchon's *The Crying of Lot 49* (1966) in Carver has been locked into the everyday atmosphere of suburban America. The domestic interiors in which his characters exist achieve the status of a cultural icon proffering nothing less than the metaphysics of emptiness.

Clearly this distinguishes the world depicted in the stories from that America so celebrated in the novels of, say, Jack Kerouac and Ken Kesey. The tradition to which their novels belong is that which celebrates the transient and the unexpected: an America which, for all its shortcomings, allows the individual to break loose from the constrictions of an environment in which the terms of existence are set. The detail of everyday life is given over to the larger rhythms and possibilities of American myth as sustained through the road, the car, and an always promised alternative: the effervescent new beginning to which any number of Huckleberry Finns endlessly move. Such aspects in Carver are seen as at once obtuse and sapping: fictions which create an alternative imaginative space in order to displace the imminent emptiness and constriction which his protagonists face. Carver's world never offers an escape route. Although the fictional world is, like Carver's own life, full of mobility, transience becomes part of a larger condition of displacement rather than celebration. To be 'on the move' is to inhabit a closing of personal space. There is no rhetoric of freedom, much less of beginnings. 'On the road' reflects a community of lost lives: a painful charting of waste and pain. No matter how or where his characters travel, the primary movement is inwards, towards a found emptiness: an interior condition beyond the words of its own naming. Movement is reduced to a necessary negotiation between the grand, but empty, gestures of cultural rhetoric and the strained, but meaningful, inflection of individual human detail and moments. The lives he traces image existences *sans* the saving rhetoric of Huck, McMurphy, or Dean Moriarty. Space, as such, is more akin to the personal geometries noted in Sam Shepard's *Motel Chronicles* (1982) and given such forceful poetic import in the Wim Wender's film, for which Shepard wrote the screenplay: *Paris, Texas* (1985).

3

In this sense the often noted influence of Hemingway on Carver's work remains problematic. As he admitted, 'On occasion it's been said that my writing is "like" Hemingway's writing. But I can't say his writing influenced mine.'[13] Although Hemingway remains 'one of many' who have had an effect on Carver's work, there is often a sense of similarity between them: the spareness, the flat tones, even the subject-matter seem to establish a distinct ambience between the two fictional worlds. And yet there is a qualitative difference which, once again, establishes the particular terms on which Carver depicts his contemporary America. Just as Carver empties and opens up the contingencies of American myth, so he exposes the extent to which the Hemingway code is dependent upon it. As such Carver moves between the two: a mythic past gauged against a banal and yet menacing present, reinvesting meaning in a Hemingway style now devoid of its myth-making prerogatives. Hemingway's codes of identity become little more than projections of fantasy and popular myth which hide the cultural *nada* beneath. Hemingway sanitized.

Thus hunting and fishing, as in Hemingway, figure as basic subjects in many Carver stories, but they do so from the perspective of a suburban America in which male codes exist only as part of a larger weekend ritual played out amidst family life, credit cards and mortgages. Characters equip themselves for an archetypal escape to the woods not so much à la Thoreau as à la television, film and advertising: in search of imagined selves and an imaginary America. The 'reality', of course, is different. As Michael Foley has suggested, Carver's stories

> significantly extend the Hemingway tradition into family life. In Hem's world your great love and baby die in childbirth, leaving you with despair instead of the indignities chronicled [in Carver]—work (or lack of it), bills, marital rows, screaming babies, difficult children.[14]

Look, for example, at the following extracts. The first is from Hemingway's 'Big Two-Hearted River: II' (*In Our Time* (1926)), and the second from Carver's 'The Cabin' (1984), a story about a husband's weekend fishing trip to the backwoods:

> Through the deepening water, Nick waded over to the hollow log. He took the sack off, over his head, the trout flopping as

it came out of water, and hung it so the trout were deep in the water. Then he pulled himself up on the log and sat, the water from his trousers and boots running down into the stream. He laid his rod down, moved along to the shady end of the log and took the sandwiches out of his pocket. He dipped the sandwiches in the cold water. The current carried away the crumbs. He ate the sandwiches and dipped his hat full of water to drink, the water running out through his hat just ahead of his drinking.[15]

Now the Carver:

As he fished, he began to feel some of the old excitement coming back. He kept on fishing. After a time he waded out and sat down on a rock with his back against a log. He took out the cookies. He wasn't going to hurry anything. Not today. A flock of small birds flew from across the river and perched on some rocks close to where he was sitting. They rose when he scattered a handful of crumbs toward them. The tops of the trees creaked and the wind was drawing the clouds up out of the valley and over the hills. Then he heard a spatter of shots from somewhere in the forest across the river.[16]

Characteristically Hemingway associates himself with his 'hero'. In Carver there is none of this; or at least if there is, it is borne out of a shared sense of desperation. Indeed, Hemingway's celebration of Nick's act of fishing in solitary splendour is compounded by the way in which the language establishes an implied unity of experience. Nature here is a surrounding presence and pulls Nick into its flux and encircling processes. The water is 'deepening' as Nick too moves deeper into this 'other'. As such the smallest movement infers a larger ritual. The verbs celebrate individual activity as part of an assumed sanctity of action, as Nick redefines himself in relation to the elements in which he is immersed: 'pulled', 'running', 'moved' and 'dipped' constitute an essential language of being. Equally, individual objects take upon themselves the status of religious icons—most obviously the rod as key to a larger code of meaning vested in the myth of male individualism. Each act by Nick reinscribes his part within the larger unity: an ideal purity of being in which American man is wholly free from social, historical and political complications. The American self, so to speak, is immersed in American nature. Nick is alone; he is not lost. If the water is cold, it is not uncomfortable. Rather this is symbolic of a purity as key to the larger communion. Such moments in Hemingway are not only characteristic of his philosophy; they are offered as achieved epiphanies which give sudden meaning to his heroes' existential condition and exist as the direct opposite to the *nada* of 'A Clean Well-Lighted Place'.

In the Carver extract the effect is quite different. The ritual and assumed unity of being is wholly absent just as the prose undercuts any attempt on the part of the character to refer his actions to larger patterns of meaning. The fiction, so to speak, deconstructs the codifying myths even as it re-inscribes them into a context which exposes their pretensions to significance. Fishing here is no more than an attempt on the part of the character to play out the Hemingway myth. Carver undercuts the effect by the merest detail. The mention of 'cookies', for example, has such a presence. Just as the world would be wholly inappropriate in the Hemingway, it is wholly appropriate in the Carver, even though both authors describe similar situations and landscapes. The cookies here are from the supermarket with their ingredients printed on the side of the packet. One equally imagines that any fish the protagonist might catch are from the freezer compartment: gutted and breaded for the microwave. Fishing, as such, is part of a recreational activity, not an existential code of being.

The other aspects of the fishing trip in 'The Cabin' become part of an equally empty construction (or reconstruction) of a mythic America. The 'cabin' is just that; not part of a wilderness habitat but a motel which advertises its accommodation by a 'flickering neon sign'. On sale are moccasins alongside 'Indian bead necklaces and bracelets and pieces of petrified wood'. On the wall is 'A big Frederic Remington reproduction'.[17] The 'cabin', as such, takes upon itself an imaginative space which seeks to re-create a lost America through fantasy and dream; it exists as a

minor (and run-down) version of Disneyland and Disney-
world: a museum culture in which the promise of the
culture's myths are given an immediate and seemingly central
significance.

But Carver gives to the situation a characteristic twist
which cuts straight through the surface fantasy. Mr. Harrold,
the fisherman, becomes embroiled in a real hunt as ferocious
as anything to be found in Hemingway. The sudden turn
in pace—signalled by the spatter of shots at the end of the
extract—is characteristic of the eruption of actual violence
into a world previously distanced through the comfort of
myth and fabrication. At such moments Carver is able to
establish a sense of menace and imminent danger which
reveals a frightening and brutal dimension to the culture.
Within seconds of his character eating his cookie a band of
rough-necks has descended on him and he has a 'barrel'
pointed directly at his stomach. 'Nature' is now a nightmare. This is the man who lounged in his cabin reading
'old *Life* magazines' before fishing. The river now is not
Hemingway's big two-hearted river; it is 'impossibly cold'
with a 'heart-stopping cold water'. Mr. Harrold is, ironically,
a fish out of water. As his fantasy enters the horrible reality
of imminent blood-letting, so 'He begins to think of home,
of getting back there before dark.' He chooses the very
world which is anathema to the Hemingway hero. Mr.
Harrold seeks the certainties, not of ritual, but of complacency and has been forced to confront the terms on which
his own life is lived: as a series of fictions which belie the
reality they would image. In the end to go home is, for
him, to return not so much to a welcoming habitat as to a
frightening lie, for in the space of a few moments the
basis of his world has been blown apart. He is lost in
America.

Many of Carver's stories involve such a moment of recognition and insight in which the fictions by which we live are
viciously wiped out. Characters find themselves looking into
a void: desperate in their attempts to understand such sudden and disastrous knowledge. If the terms of this revelation
are most often within suburban life, it is realized in a quite
different way to similar crises in, say, the writing of John

Cheever and John Updike. At such moments in Carver, relationships freeze and wither. Communication seems impossible as we observe couples in a *mise-en-scène* of unqualified
knowledge about their lives. Reality, so to speak, breaks in
upon lives held together by the most fragile of myths and
illusions.

'So Much Water so Close to Home' (1977) is such a
story. Again we are in Hemingway country: a fishing trip
by a group of male suburbanites out for the weekend.
This is predominantly a male world whose members 'play
poker, bowl, and fish together'—the stuff of any number
of American films and soap operas. 'They are decent men,
family men, responsible at their jobs' and yet, as in James
Dickey's *Deliverance* (1970), their attempts to play out the
myth of a rugged America go frighteningly wrong as upon
their arrival in the woods they discover the dead body of a
young girl. She had been raped, murdered, and her body
thrown into the river. But they do not report their discovery
to the police; not at once anyway, for that would upset their
weekend plans to fish and camp. Instead they bring the body
to the riverbank:

> One of the men, I don't know who, it might have been Stuart,
> he could have done it, waded into the water and took the girl
> by the fingers and pulled her, still face down, closer to shore,
> into shallow water, and then took a piece of nylon cord and
> tied it around her wrist and then secured the cord to tree roots,
> all the while the flashlights of the other men played over the
> girl's body. Afterwards, they went back to camp and drank
> more whisky. Then they went to sleep. The next morning,
> Saturday, they cooked breakfast, drank lots of coffee, more
> whisky, and then split up to fish, two men upriver, two men
> down.[18]

This is not simply a story about moral complacency on the
part of a group of men crassly indifferent to what they have
found. Rather, Carver's prose suggests a complex series of
moral issues which the discovery prompts. The language, for
example, has quasi-sexual undertones. The lamps 'play' over
the girl's body as her naked state is made openly available to
the voyeuristic gaze of the men's eyes. Similarly the way the

body is tied (trussed) up and touched suggests a prurient form of male fantasy. After the 'show' they return to feeding themselves with drink and food. The reality of their situation has dissolved, the terms of the girl's death forgotten. What emerges is a disturbing portrayal of moral numbness and grossness. They seem blind and indifferent to what has happened to the girl; a whole area of moral awareness has been lost.

Crucially, however, Carver's use of a female first-person narrative voice (the wife of Stuart, one of the men involved) radically alters the way we judge the men's actions, for it is the effect they have upon *her* that becomes so significant. Their actions are thus deflected via a female consciousness which reports on the implications of this male ethos. As such (and it is the wife who goes to the girl's funeral and looks at her face in the coffin) the narrative voice opens up a distance between wife and husband which recasts the men's crassness in relation to larger codes and cultural assumptions. The husband has become someone unrecognizable in what the episode has revealed about him as an individual. What makes it so characteristic of Carver is the way such knowledge frames their relationship through a series of looks. The wife attempts to take the measure of a partner now strangely different. Her eyes scan him in order to know. Silence is everything. As she looks so an entire history of thwarted feeling floods in to fill what is now the emptiness of their marriage. The wife 'hates him', but even so, 'We will go on and on and on and on. We will go on even now, as if nothing had happened. I look at him across the picnic table with such intensity that his face drains.' Carver is not so much interested in laying blame on anybody as dramatizing the extent to which the couple, even with such knowledge, are caught in a seemingly unresolvable moral and private conundrum; for the incident brings into focus the terms of their lives, and it is this which frightens them. When, at the end, the husband declares his love for his wife, Carver is able to make a simple statement resonate with ferocious but pathetic meaning. As they remain frozen in time, and locked in silence, so we sense their emptiness; Carver has pictured their histories and, in so doing, made their lives icons of a larger condition and, by implication, culture.

4

One of the significant aspects of this story is the extent to which Carver brings the mythology of the American wilderness into the living rooms of the American suburb: thus the reason why so much water *is* so close to home. But this, in turn, underlines the extent to which virtually all of the short stories are set within the landscape of suburban America. The space of a Carver story is invariably an interior, be it kitchen, bathroom, bedroom, or living room. These are private spaces, but they are also limited habitats: closed areas of movement and contact so that the outside world seems to enter most often through the television. Indeed it is central to this story that the couple see the girl's murder reported on T.V. As the husband is 'in his leather recliner chair' and the wife 'on the sofa with a blanket and magazine', so 'a voice cuts into the program to say that the murdered girl has been identified.'

Television is a constant presence in the world of Carver's characters and the archetypal Carver environment is saturated with the apparatus and paraphernalia of modern electronic communication. In houses and apartments where virtually nothing is said, much less heard, lives are filled with the noise of T.V.s, radios, ringing telephones and record players. And yet their presence points up the extent to which these domestic interiors seem isolated within the terms of their individual boundaries. Rather than establish any sense of continuity or communication with an external world, so telephones disrupt lives and T.V.s flatten and make unreal events beyond the home. In 'Put yourself in my Shoes', for example, 'The telephone rang' while a character is 'running the vacuum cleaner'. On answering it he is told that an acquaintance had 'shot himself in the mouth'.[19] Similarly a story entitled 'Whoever Was Using this Bed' (from *Elephant*) has a woman phoning a couple to ask about a person about whom they have never heard. The call throws the relationship into sudden chaos, as it plays off the characters' insecurities and phobias. One's home is not immune from the outside. The telephone becomes an intrusive instrument, almost menacing in its power to disrupt and unsettle the lives of others.[20] And yet paradoxically it is the main bearer of news, for people do not receive letters in Carver's America; they receive junk mail. In a story centred on a postman ('What do you do in San Fransisco') we are told that he delivers catalogues from Sears, Western Autos flyers, and insurance plans. There are, as it were, no letters. The significance of such a state would not have been lost on Melville's Bartleby.

And similarly with the T.V. (rather than television). T.V.s in Carver abound, emphasizing the extent to which these American homes and environments are seemingly bombarded with images of other communities, personalities and world events. And yet there is rarely any awareness of an outside world in Carver. People are locked into the terms of their own lives. The television in Carver empties events of significance and historical contexts. All exists with equal status because all has become part of a single stream of images. There is no reality, so to speak, beyond the screen. The T.V. exists as a form of symbiotic national icon devoid of any moral reference. It spews its animated images into domestic interiors giving events the same status as a pattern in the carpet.

At times, of course, T.V. underlines an individual's loneliness and isolation. In 'Preservation', for example, an unemployed husband gives his days over to looking at T.V. When his wife returns one afternoon:

> She could hear the TV going in the living room as she let herself in the door to the kitchen. The coffee pot was on the stove, and the burner was on low. From where she stood in the kitchen, holding her purse, she could look into the living room and see the back of the sofa and the TV screen. Figures moved across the screen. Her husband's bare feet stuck out from one end of the sofa. At the other end, on a pillow which lay across the arm of the sofa, she could see the crown of his head. He didn't stir.[21]

Here a minimum of description achieves a density of effect as, seemingly, an entire life is imaged before us. Not a word is spoken; Carver has pictured a relationship for us without describing the individuals involved. The achievement is a marvellously felt image of emptiness, paradoxically framed and given meaning by the overwhelming presence of the T.V. There is a surreal otherness about such a moment. Even though she could 'hear the T.V. going' the effect is one of silence. Nothing can, nor need, be said. The stasis of the figure, and the wife's observation of her husband, are given credence precisely because we are so aware of the 'figures' which 'moved across the screen'.

T.V. here is almost an ur-form for the age and, as such, is given a presence appropriate to a culture which has made it basic to any domestic environment. And its presence is endless. People do not read newspapers in Carver's fiction, much less books (or short stories). If they do read, they look at the latest catalogues from Sears. Much less, of course, do they talk. Ironically the T.V. becomes the focus of communal activity. People eat in its presence, hold conversations whilst watching it, even meet whilst it is on. And yet rarely does it register as anything other than a background noise (and clue to a pervasive meaninglessness). People, in effect, do not watch it. They 'hear a T.V. going'. In Britain we would say that the television is 'on'. In Carver the T.V. is 'going', suggestive of an endless, almost random and unregistered transmission of images as part of a larger unreality. Thus no one in the end watches T.V.; they sit in front of it, dazed by its capacity to produce infinite images and oblivious to the chaos it reflects.

Carver's distinctive awareness of T.V., however, is quite different from, say, Jerzy Kosinski's use of it in *Being There* (1971). In that novel the central character, a naïve gardener called Chance, is wholly dominated by a sense of T.V. which constructs and determines the world he assumes to be real. In contrast Carver's use of T.V. reflects the world his characters inhabit, not a world they have created. It is a world in which, if life inside the house is often meaningless and frozen, then life outside the house is equally meaningless and confused. T.V. thus empties history and world events, leaving them without depth and resonance: so, 'In the living room Walter Conkrite/ prepares us for the moon shot.'[22]

History as a series of discrete and knowable events no longer exists. Rather, everything is viewed as if on T.V.; figures and rooms are glimpsed as if on television screens, reduced to little more than a surface effect. The effect is that suggested by Jean Baudrillard in *America* (1988) when he notes that in the States the T.V. is 'often to be seen functioning like an hallucination in the empty room of houses or hotel rooms . . .'. At such moments 'the TV reveals itself for what is really is: a video of another world, ultimately addressed to no one at all, delivering its images indifferently, indifferent to its own messages. . . .'[23]

One can understand, then, why Carver's settings have been so compared to the paintings of Edward Hopper. Hopper's images of solitary figures and couples cast amidst an array of empty rooms and environments seem to speak directly to the world Carver's characters inhabit. Indeed, the space each depicts—apartments, motel rooms, offices, diners, and cars—evinces a particular kind of American loneliness which borders on pathos. No one, so to speak, has a home in Hopper. *Night Hawks* (1942), a seminal Hopper painting, could be a definitive image for Carver's own world of displaced persons.

The difference is that Carver's stories are usually set in the protagonists' homes. The space in which we see their loneliness is their only refuge: the single space in which they can, paradoxically, be themselves. In such a condition they move between these individual areas of retreat to extreme locations in which different orders of fantasy are played out (cabins, forests, etc.). Between the two they seem not to exist, even when on the road they are isolated in their cars. Highways as such occupy a vacuum. We never have the sense of moving through a landscape or of travelling through cities and palpable communities. There seems no America, as it were, to know, much less touch. Thus, once again, the sense of menace and, often, of strangeness and dread. Lives are cast amidst an overpowering sense of emptiness: what Eugene Goodheart referred to as a 'quality of surreal menace that never quite materialises'.[24] In the end perhaps the appropriate comparison is not so much with the paintings of Hopper as with the full-sized figure-sculptures of George Segal. As in Segal's work Carver's stories achieve the extraordinary effect of characters frozen in a kind of pantomime. They stand, sit, or muse alone, fixed in chairs or glimpsed through doors and windows which give to their existence a deliberate and unknowable otherness. What the stories seek, like Segal's sculptures, is to render the terms of that condition with an intensity which borders on the poetic: a felt sense of pathos and loss. In this sense nothing, indeed, need happen in a Carver story. They are able to encapsulate a history, and a life, in the merest detail, gesture, or moment, a *mise-en-scène* of America in the last quarter of the twentieth century: individual states which resonate across the continent with the force of a moral picturing.

From the perspective of their domestic interiors so the stories turn on a pin, or rather a comma. The hesitant pause between two people can open up a gulf, or reveal an interior neither wishes to see. And this, it seems to me, is the especial resonance of Carver's so-called spareness. It achieves its power through a singular weighing of each syllable on the page. Eugene Goodheart is correct to call Carver a 'lyric poet' (in his stories); but it is a lyricism borne of silence and hiatuses. A vacuum, ultimately, in which middle America is figured. A state of existence in which a story exists as 'wobbling in the air for all to hear'.

5

Raymond Carver's last collection of stories, *Elephant*, published in the year he died, ends with a story concerning the death of a major influence on his work: Anton Chekhov. Indeed one reviewer felt the influence to be so significant as to call him the 'American Chekhov'.[25] And yet 'Errand' could not be further from the usual world of the stories. Set in Europe at the turn of the century it follows the final period of Chekhov's life: seemingly an homage to Carver's Russian mentor. But the effect of 'Errand' is to gradually erase Chekhov as the centre of attention as the ethos underpinning Carver's American stories takes over. Chekhov is claimed for middle America.

Thus as the story develops we leave the formal grandeur

of the opening section involving a lengthy gourmet meal at the 'best restaurant' in Moscow (the absolute opposite to the T.V. dinners so many of his American characters eat), and move to the bare details of the room in which Chekhov dies from tuberculosis. Equally, as I noted above, the story displaces Leo Tolstoy, as almost metaphorically expunging both Tolstoy's sense of the novel and of his personal philosophy as alien to Carver's world. Indeed both Chekhov and Tolstoy are eclipsed as the story increasingly focuses upon a hotel waiter who, having brought a bottle of champagne to the room where Chekhov is dying, notices on his return that the cork is on the floor. It is this detail which concerns him, and us, so that the implications of Chekhov's death are, effectively, forgotten. Carver reveals in 'Errand' an almost effortless shift of attention, more and more displacing the historical circumstances of Chekhov's death in favour of his own fiction. In essence it becomes the waiter's story. Chekhov, ironically, ends as an intruder who happened to be at the hotel. And thus the extent to which the story is so centrally Carver, for the waiter, like the figures in Carver's American stories, has been made visible: photographed, so to speak, as a singular being within a life as distinctive as the other characters in the story. It is the waiter upon whom we focus; and, of course, the champagne cork. In a recent anthology Paul Theroux suggested that one of the strengths of the short story is its ability to suggest a novel in the space of three or four pages.[26] The difference with Carver is that the merest detail can contain not just a story, nor even a novel, but an entire life and history, and we are made to feel the significance of that detail amidst the complicating contingencies of a larger condition at once social, cultural and moral: as much private as public and as much interior as exterior. In 'Errand', with the waiter in the room and the 'mortician' attending to Chekhov's body, Olga, Chekhov's widow, asks the waiter to leave. 'Will you go?' she asks:

> But at that moment the young man was thinking of the cork still resting near the toe of his shoe. To retrieve it he would have to bend over, still gripping the vase. He would do this. He leaned over. Without looking down, he reached out and closed it into his hand.[27]

119

And thus the narrative closes. 'Errand' is a story which seems to privilege the seen over the spoken and, in a story so concerned with Chekhov, makes every use of the pause, the hesitant moment, and the sense of nuance beneath the simplest act. In the end (like Chekhov) Carver gives precedence to the silent over the spoken and, inevitably, lays stress on the seen rather than the heard. And yet it is the play between these two worlds which makes them part of the continuing enigma Carver seeks to picture: a condition in which, while nothing can be said, everything might be glimpsed.

6

In the end, of course, one insists that there are other Americas besides Carver's and that, for all its intensity and precision, his perspective reduces everything to a single condition. But perhaps this is the point, for in coming to Carver we should not read his stories so much as read *a* story: one at a time, inching along the prose in order to take in its exact measurement. The stories, in other words, depend for their effect on a sense of both isolation and singularity. As such they depict a common world made unique. To read them at speed and in succession is to return their subjects to precisely the surface gloss and glaze depicted on all of those T.V. screens. To read them hesitantly and sparingly is to retain the separateness of each life which, in the end, becomes a celebration of their singularity. And yet Carver's world is very much black and white. Unlike the T.V.s his characters view, there is little sense of colour. But once again the absence of colour is part of the achievement, for the stories drain the lives of surface effect and cover. They do not reflect a world we would prefer to see; they reflect a world in its essence. Thus they confront the reader with a kind of ambivalent complexity. Perhaps this is why, in the end, Carver is closer to James than he is to Hemingway. The difference is, of course, that Carver achieves a syntax amidst a fragmented reality born of silence. As in 'My Father's Life', an entire life can reverberate through a single word:

I listened to people say consoling things to my mother, and I was glad that my dad's family had turned up, had come to where he was. I thought I'd remember everything that was said and done that day and maybe find a way to tell it sometime. But I didn't. I forgot it all, or nearly. What I do remember is that I heard our name used a lot that afternoon, my dad's name and mine. But I knew they were talking about my dad. *Raymond*, these people kept saying in their beautiful voices out of my childhood. *Raymond.*[28]

Presence and absence: the continuing ambivalence he would picture. Like the photograph of Carver on the back cover of *Elephant* he looks at us in a reciprocal gaze of intent. His image achieves a singular presence endlessly absent. It is, in other words, the archetypal Carver predicament—investing the glimpse in what can only be a syntax of silence: the continuing attempt to render what, in the end, is a very particular kind of American loneliness.

NOTES

1. Michael Foley, 'Dirty Realist', *London Review of Books*, 2 May 1985, 12.
2. Eugene Goodheart, 'Raymond Carver's *Cathedral*' in *Pieces of Resistance* (Cambridge: Cambridge University Press, 1987), p. 163.
3. 'Errand' in *Elephant and Other Stories* (London: Collins Harvill, 1988), p. 113.
4. Ibid., p. 113.
5. 'My Father's Life' in *Fires* (London: Picador, 1986), p. 20.
6. Quoted in the 'Editorial' to *Dirty Realism: New Writing from America*, *Granta* x (1983), 5.
7. 'Reading' in *In a Marine Light: Selected Poems* (London: Picador, 1988), p. 138. The whole poem is of significance.
8. *Michigan Quarterly Review*, Vol. xxvi (1987), 711. Carver is one of a number of writers who share a common view of the contemporary American scene in relation to their work. These include, for example, Jayne Anne Phillips and Tobias Wolff. Of significance is that Carver's widow, Tess Gallagher (to whom much of Carver's work is dedicated) has published a collection of stories, *The Lover of Horses* (1989), which owes much to Carver's influence. See James Wood, 'From the secular side of the American miracle' in the *Guardian*, 6 April 1989, 22.

9. See 'Harley's Swans' in *In a Marine Light*, p. 75.
10. *Fires*, p. 24—but see the whole essay, 'On Writing', pp. 22–7.
11. Ibid., p. 27.
12. Ibid., p. 35. Again the whole essay, 'Fires', is significant especially in relation to influences on his writing as well as the circumstances of his life. See pp. 28–39.
13. Ibid., p. 28.
14. Foley, p. 12.
15. 'Big Two-Hearted River: II' in *The Essential Hemingway* (Harmondsworth: Penguin, 1967), p. 366.
16. 'The Cabin' in *Fires*, p. 152.
17. Frederic Remington (1861–1909) remains one of the most popular and important painters of the old West. Carver uses the reference as part of a larger inheritance which has been lost to the contemporary condition. 'Remington', as such, has now been claimed by a company: the name being of significance because of its association with a make of electric razor rather than art. It belongs to a corporate America led by Colonel Sanders and other such 'leading' names.
18. I quote from the version in *Fires*, pp. 185–204. A shorter version appears in *The Stories of Raymond Carver* (London: Picador, 1985), pp. 235–40.
19. *The Stories of Raymond Carver*, p. 101.
20. *Elephant*, pp. 27–44.
21. *The Stories of Raymond Carver*, p. 315.
22. See 'An Account' in *In a Marine Light*, pp. 164–65. The poem is concerned with Carver's sense of T.V. and finishes with the lines 'And someone thought to turn off/ the images pulsing across the screen.'
23. Jean Baudrillard, *America* (New York and London: Verso, 1988), trans. Chris Turner, p. 50.
24. *Pieces of Resistance*, p. 162.
25. Peter Kemp, 'The American Chekhov' in the *Sunday Times* (Book Section), 7 August 1988, 1–2.
26. *Sudden Fiction*, eds. Robert Shapard and James Thomas (Harmondsworth: Penguin, 1988), p. 228.
27. *Elephant*, p. 124.
28. *Fires*, p. 21.

5

'What we write about when we write about Gordon Lish'

by DAVID SEABROOK

> 'Here', said Mr. Thomson, 'is a novel ready to your hand: all
> you have to do is work up the scenery, develop the characters,
> and improve the style.'
> 'My dear fellow,' said I, 'they are just the three things that
> I would rather die than set my hand to. It shall be published
> as it stands.'
> 'But it's so bald,' objected Mr. Thomson.
> 'I believe there is nothing so noble as baldness', replied I,
> 'and I am sure there is nothing so interesting. I would have
> all literature bald, and all authors (if you like), but one.'
> 'Well, well,' said Mr. Thomson, 'we shall see.'
> —Robert Louis Stevenson, Preface to
> *The Master of Ballantrae*

1

In its Fall and Winter issues of 1988 the *Michigan Quarterly
Review* published 'A Symposium on Contemporary American Fiction': solicited contributions from more than seventy
authors on their preferences in current American writing.[1]
Many opted for brief, breathy endorsements, sometimes of
each other; a few writers, inured to interrogation, declined to
name names. Strewn through these responses is the general

rant on the subject of minimalist writing, and when the name of Gordon Lish is finally invoked it is to make the rant more specific and also to specify why he has not been mentioned before: 'The so-called "minimalist" writers—some people have called them the children of Gordon Lish—are thin, self-regarding, narcissistic. . . .'[2] Lish is the grey eminence behind this literary anorexia, the chief offender in what, elsewhere in the symposium, Raymond Carver refers to as the 'stale debate' of 'Minimalism v. Maximalism'.[3]

The term's obfuscatory appeal is strengthened, in Carver's case, by the notion that his stories are both cosmetically confounding and obscurely traditional, *à la* Hemingway, for the studied eschewal of all but the middle of a narrative is nothing less than an urbane acknowledgement of its incompleteness. Many of the symposium's contributors, in common with British and American reviewers, adopt a correspondingly traditional view of his work, assessing the deployment of computerized rigour in the service of some higher, humanistic purpose. Carver and Lish both have claims to be regarded as minimalists, yet Lish seems to have been penalized for his appropriation of the end rather than the middle. Despite the acquisition of favourable reviews at home, his is a notable absence from the *Michigan Quarterly Review*'s symposium of 'distinguished American fiction writers'; in Britain, where his short story collection remains unavailable, his name is practically unknown.[4]

Lish's early work, the short stories that form the collection *What I Know So Far* (1984), seems to blot its own letter of introduction through its forfeiture of recognizable literary aims—character, momentum, resolution—for the cultivation of a breezy anonymity. Lish's pennywise ratepayers fret over sons, wives, vagrants, and insist on their citizenhood. Yet living liaises with language to alter the status of a soliloquy and the presuppositions of its speaker: 'The wife insisted she would tell her version first. I was instantly interested because of the word' ('Everything I Know'). Conventional narration is jettisoned in favour of what can be termed literal figurations, in which narrative revelation is redefined as verbal process, whose speakers, as the sum of their sentences, bear semantic, rather than psychological scars. The content of the

stories, which concern themselves with codes, shapes, surfaces, and, of course, stories and poems, animates them as
suburban farce whilst enshrining anxiety as form. The fear is
of what will take space, not place: 'But you're looking at this
and thinking these are really truths. You're thinking why
make sentences if all they do is fool' ('Imp Among Aunts').

The resultant pressure postulates a fever chart that may be
read sociologically or psycho-semantically, as the speaker of
'The Psoriasis Diet' (*psoriasis*: 'skin disease marked by red
patches covered with scales', *O.E.D.*) is discovering:

> *Psoriasis*
> I've seen worse words. Besides, it got me on education,
> being as how I took up an interest in language right after. I
> started with all the pee-ess words and just kept on after that.
> There was no stopping me, I can tell you.
> There was no stopping it, either.

This is figuration as disfigurement in which each sentence
spoken is another skin sloughed, and in tandem with this
exfoliation Lish's own lexicon is laid waste, acceding to the
slow death of dyslexias. As the narrator declares as the voice
closes:

> Not anachronism.
> *Anachorism.*
> Look it up.

Experimentation ebbs into euthanasia, to which the reading (as writing) process is seen to be analogous. Elsewhere
the stories trumpet their demise rather more discordantly:

> It is why I am not very interested in people—nor in myself.
> We all of us know exactly what to say, and say it—the man
> who sat with me making a drama out of his half-finished glass;
> I, speaking to him then and speaking to you now; you, reading
> and making your mind up about this page.
> There is no escape from this. Nor is it any longer necessary
> to act as if there might be. ('What Is Left to Link Us')

This is the point at which the tortuous tramlines of Borgesian
legerdemain and *nouvelle roman* tendentiousness converge. A
route to nowhere, in fact. The psoriasis victim sheds tears as
well as skin.

The ascendancy of a counter-impulse discontinues this

cycle of the self-defining dilemma. Lish flees claustrality and consecrates a structuralist shibboleth in a deferral to his reader as writer, surfacing in Ian Hamilton's bedevilled biography of J. D. Salinger as a parenthetical footnote to a legend when the book's rubble of conjecture finally yields an *aperçu* of genuine interest:

> There have been Salinger spoofs: in 1977 *Esquire* published a story called 'For Rupert—With No Promises' and there were rumours that Salinger had written it (the piece was actually composed by the magazine's fiction editor, Gordon Lish). . . .[5]

'Spoof' sits oddly in the story's proximity; the wheedling and wonder of Salinger's style is cleaved to down to the high-school italics, yet the virulence of its refutation makes it more taunt that treat. In an address to his brother's son the narrator Buddy warns him of imminent danger at the hands of his father, the terminally ill Smithy. Adamant that his ex-wife has poisoned the teenager against him, he fears for the life of 5-year-old Rupert, his second and best-loved boy: 'Some way none of us can predict, my firstborn will stalk my second, find a way to hurt *him* because my death *robs* him of his chance to hurt *me*.' Murder is the proposed solution 'and if you are your father's son, Chap, you will see he has a point'.

'For Rupert' begins its assault on the Salinger code with Buddy's commendations of 'a Viennese logician', presumably Wittgenstein, as a prelude to his brother's 'reasoned argument', whose obeisance to the dictates of logic 'could give the Viennese logician cards and spades'. The wayward mysticism of Salinger's Glass family is then called briskly to heel by the Old Testament authority of Lish's scenario, which offers 'No Promises', of reprieve or anything else. It is perhaps the voice of a readership (the readership that thought it was reading Salinger) appalled at its own assertiveness in the face of such desertion.

'For Jerome—with Love and Kisses' counters the logical proposition with the emotional outburst. Chicago meat importer Sol Salinger does not expect another novel, a telephone call will suffice. 'Please God, Heaven should make a miracle and your father should live that long, you won't have to worry, his number is in the book.' Hyperbolic, semetic musicality stresses family ties and the story does service as a trenchant rebuttal of Kafka's 'Letter to his Father', orphaning a parent into a jeremiad of his own in which anonymity shades sleekly into stature. Lish broadens the plain man's philosophy of his speakers to encompass the philistinism of the cultural entrepreneur; Sol takes the eponymous liberty with his son's name, for as the European 'Jerome' he is better placed for the Nobel Prize: 'A medal! Thousands and thousands of dollars and a medal!'

Lish's exploitation of the public face of American letters forms the cornerstone of his achievement here and in his first novel, *Dear Mr. Capote* (1983). The novel interprets that arena's formidable, at times causal, link between public profile and *oeuvre* as schism, and schizophrenia. The reader writes to be read by the writer in an act of mutual publicity that is also a severance of the self from its expression: the primacy of reading over writing, silence over speech, is both pre-empted and pre-ordained. The speech of the people mutates, in Lish, into a self-cancelling babble whose warmest desire is aphasia. The narrator of his second novel *Peru* (1986) takes time off to plead: 'I have been waiting for God to reach down and make me stop saying these things.'

Peru fractures the familiar address of the nuclear family man to the average reader into a set of fresh disjunctions, pitting the absolution of action against the guilt of transcription, consequently transferred to the reader as the non-communication of pure style: 'Maybe it will be a curse on you for just hearing all of this.' His achievement in these novels is recorded as unprecedented disaster.

2

You could be forgiven for thinking, on reading Gerald Clarke's biography, that Truman Capote's life formed a strenuous social round of invitations and defamations punctuated at intervals by the odd book.[6] To his credit, Clarke dwells at some length upon the odd book, charting the six years of research and preparation for *In Cold Blood* (1965). Its completion was delayed as he awaited the execution of the two murderers. Dick Hickock and Perry Smith were so successful at prolonging their stay of execution that Capote began to doubt that they would ever hang. They remained alive long enough to discover the book's projected title, with its announcement of premeditated murder—an imputation both vigorously denied—and grew anxious concerning their portrayal in the 'novel'. Smith asked rather pointedly in a letter to his chronicler, 'What is the purpose of this book?'[7]

Capote sympathized. As Clarke reveals, although he regarded Hickock as a cheap opportunist, Smith seems to have taken on the lineaments of an *alter ego*. Another stunted Southern orphan, Smith was keen to educate himself, and welcomed presents of books. Clarke quotes from the tortuous mandarin of his correspondence with Capote, and even includes a poem.[8] Capote and Smith formed a remorseless pair: the high-minded novelist straining every nerve for the common touch, and the killer who aspired to Parnassus. At times, it seems, Smith cherished his mentor, and at others quite the reverse: 'Flexing his weight-lifter's muscles during one interview, he pointed out to Truman that he could kill him in a minute, before a guard could come to his rescue.'[9]

Clarke provides a full account of the novel's fulsome reception, as he does of the *Answered Prayers* controversy which occurred some ten years later.[10] In 1959, shortly after the publication of *Breakfast at Tiffany's* (1958), Norman Mailer had remarked presciently in *Advertisements for Myself* that

> I would suspect he [Capote] hesitates between the attractions of Society . . . and the novel he could write of the gossip column's real life, a major work, but it would banish him forever from his favourite world.[11]

In 1975 'La Cote Basque, 1965' appeared in the November edition of *Esquire*. A baroquely barbed portrait of New York's élite, Capote intended it as a foretaste of a massive Proustian enterprise that would silence critics and victims for good and all. In the weeks that followed publication, friends shunned him and the model for his murderess, Ann Hopkins, died of an overdose. Everything seemed to be going according to plan. Yet Capote himself was—or claimed to be—devastated: 'But they knew I was a writer. I don't understand it.'[12] But by the time 'Unspoiled Monsters', the final chapter extant of *Answered Prayers*, appeared in *Esquire* in 1976 he was beginning to warm to the rôle of malefactor. Toting a stiletto and garbed in pall-bearer black, he eyes us forbiddingly from the magazine's cover: writer turned Ripper, an exiled man.

Capote's decline (in most senses of the word) was fairly rapid in the years that followed and hindsight tells us that the collection of fan letters published in 1983 arrived absurdly late. But who could deny him his past?

'La Cote Basque'. Wasn't that what you called it? What a title! It says a mouthful. Watch out! Here it comes! It's just a person writing, but it's the wave, run for your lives!

I was just wondering. You think I could use it instead of one of them from the calendar? How about instead of *capstone*? 'La Cote Basque'. So what do you think? You think it would work? . . . You think it would open up her eyes?

Dear Mr. Capote is the first novel by the former fiction editor at *Esquire* who accepted 'La Cote Basque' for publication, and his narrator is a New York bank clerk who has killed twenty-three women and who wants to negotiate with Capote concerning his memoirs. Here he ponders the efficacy of 'La Cote Basque' with a view to his twenty-fourth victim: would the mention of it open her left eye wide enough to permit the insertion of Paki (Pakistan with the blade unfolded) into its pupil? Has it retained its power to shock?

Dear Mr. Capote is replete with such satirical moments—the Cote Basque is where the narrator wants to conduct negotiations when they finally meet; *In Cold Blood* is still a classic; but then again, 'a handful of farmers and they're all in the same family and none of it happened on ice!'—and in some respects it is possible to regard the book as a fable on literary stardom.

As such, it is heartwarmingly effective: the narrator discovers early on that his wife shares her initials with the great man ('Tamara Chris and Mr. Truman Capote!') and a lot later

129

that the names Norman (Mailer) and Truman contain the same word ('It just hit me like a ton of bricks'). Yet the novel's possibilities reach beyond the exquisitely satirical. On the second page Capote is informed that Mailer, another laureate of Death Row in *The Executioner's Song* (1979), nearly got the job of ghost-writer but he 'muffed it'. So we begin reading, with the realization that this might easily have been *Dear Mr. Mailer*, yet, as the novel progresses—or rather, as we become more accustomed to what the book *is*—we are able to dismiss the concept of an alternative correspondent as unfeasible. It is the pixillated Southerner who is the object of desire.

Lish's narrator (unnamed in the book, although the blurb refers to him as David) bears an interesting family resemblance to Capote's Perry Smith. Another orphaned self-educator, he avails himself of a Word-a-Day calendar in order to increase his word power. In *In Cold Blood* Smith's word hoard resides within the covers of his personal dictionary and that is mainly where it stays, the killer as gagged as his victims by Capote's Flaubertian pretensions. Lish's novel is unhampered by such concerns, and an *embarras de richesses* of clichés, tautologies, archaisms and misquotes announces 'David's' autonomy in terms no Francophile can fail to grasp.

'What is the purpose of this book?' We can begin to appreciate Perry Smith's predicament as, helpless, he awaits literary judgement in his prison cell. In order to be immortalized in fiction, he must needs taste the hemp in reality: Capote had witnesses to dispose of. After numerous appeals, Smith and Hickock were finally hanged in the early hours of 14 April 1965. *In Cold Blood* was then hurriedly completed, appearing later that year in the *New Yorker* and in book form in 1966. Henceforth Perry Smith stands, according to Clarke, 'alongside Roger Chillingworth in Hawthorne's *The Scarlet Letter,* Claggart in Melville's *Billy Budd* . . .', as soon as, of course, he had included himself out.[13]

Like his real-life cousin, Lish's narrator also writes letters to Capote. Unlike Smith's, these are met with silence. Capote's presence can be discerned in the white spaces between the bulletins, an achievement Flaubert himself would have deferred to. For 'David' is reader, writer, killer and celebrity in one; in his pleas for a formal, sanitized account of his activities he proffers a reality at the point of interpretation; his biographer becomes his readership. Unlike Perry Smith, he is in the enviable position of electing to love the thing he has killed.

His chosen route to fame illuminates his purpose. 'Effectuate', for example, is 'one of the words so far' and also one of the *words* so far. Say the word—normally borrowed from the Word-a-Day calendar—and as the eyes widen insert Paki into the *left* pupil, 'since for the media you are definitely crazy if you do not stick to your trademark', and death is instantaneous, thus cancelling the possibility of interpretation. Language is experience, the word made steel.

In his biography Clarke makes no mention of the novel, though Lish is favoured with a brief appearance in which he recollects his delight in publishing 'La Cote Basque'.[14]

3

Being a killer is a bit like being a novelist. Both activities are forms of excommunication in which only one person lives to tell the tale, and the comparison loses some of its insouciance when we consider that novels themselves can prove murderous, as the furore over Salman Rushdie's The Satanic Verses has showed, and as in recent history with the courtroom claim of John Lennon's killer that Salinger's The Catcher in the Rye (1951) furnished an explanation of his action, a claim that neither Lennon's nor Salinger's biographer has condescended to record.[15] Having flourished in a state of prelapsarian bliss for thirty years as a talisman against adulthood for every nation's youth Salinger's novel (as much as its hero, Holden Caulfield) lost its own innocence abruptly and messily and took its place in the grown-up world of guilt and remorse. The apparent eccentricity of the choice made by Mark Chapman, Lennon's killer, is validated by the plausibility of the punishment, for in this sense the novel, like the singer, is killed off, murdered for being an accessory in a murder case, a figuration literalized in the context of the Rushdie controversy when public burnings of his novel took place in West Yorkshire and Greater Manchester in January 1989.

The epistolary form of Lish's novel centralizes this opposition between killer and victim. 'David's' private correspondence with Capote is characterized by a concern with mass-market sensationalism and, in accordance with tradition, the public is the intended readership permitted to intercept the messages. And yet *Dear Mr. Capote* subverts the example of, say, Samuel Richardson's *Pamela* (1740–42) by prinking out formal anachronism as stylistic innovation. Richardson's discovery of form is attended to novelistically for the first time. Originally proffered as a moral corrective to improper romances, it was not slow to commit its own improprieties, secreting a prurience that this modern descendant experiences as a complex, an anxiety over a form that is incomplete, unprepared, inferior, simply not right. Begging letters these, praying for an author's absolution. Richardson's readers derived not a little *schadenfreude* from his everlasting evocations of innocence under threat, the perpetration of *frisson*, equivocation, foreplay finally closed by narrative convention as routinely as the peephole to a floorshow—sad but supportable. Lish's book advances no narrative yet its narrative advances, its solidity and tension tumescence itself as the present suppurates in the toils of the past historic:

> I feel her getting my pants open. I see the cracks in the boards over my head. I know she is getting ready to do something. But I don't know what it is. I can see the cracks and the people go over them. I can see the shoes go over the cracks. I can feel her breath you-know-where. It's breath where I never felt it before.
>
> I can't help it. It's giving me this big boner. It's terrible having what I am telling about, and then you can't ever have it anymore.
>
> Oh, Mr. Capote, Janet Rose!

The novel raises and rears the question of intimacy in the epistolary form. Capote, far from being the cherished confidant(e) of eighteenth-century efforts, is almost wholly unknown to his correspondent, bodied forth as a media gew-gaw fit for public appropriation. I remarked earlier

'What we write about when we write about Gordon Lish'

the ways in which the narrator revenges himself upon his hero, a process by which the book is itself victimized. The disjunction between speech and form is figured in 'David's' relationship to Capote as that between the self and its expression: the book expresses a wish to become the new self of the 'non-fiction' novel. Like a planchette out of patience, its own closure, manically divergent from its prototype's, gesticulates the impossibility of closure, coherence, or change:

> You know what all of you are? You are just me talking to me and myself in the glass of a fucking oven!
> You hear me T.C.? You took him away! But you're just me and he's just me—and when I sign off, you're all just fucking nothing!
> You hear me, all you sons of bitches in your fancy fucking famous places? You're fucking nobody because I am who you are! . . .

The denial of this self muzzles the book into acceptance of its final silence, a solution rather than a completion. Language relived is duly relieved.

4

> You know what she once predicted?
> She said that even if I owned someday, she said that it wouldn't matter, that never in my life would I ever actually forget the fact that we were a family who rented. (*Peru*)

Social factors keen like furies through these works: deprivation, domestic discord, the underclass's belief in the redemptive power of lucre (Lish's characters catalogue prices of anything from egg rolls to hypothetical taxi tips with the kind of painful commitment Dos Passos brings to *U.S.A.*'s treatment of the Depression) and, above all, the question of status: at home, at work and down in the sandbox, where, as *Peru*'s plaintive narrator has discovered,

> even if nobody had gone ahead and said so to begin with, still and all, there was always a winner, there was always a

133

winner, and the loser knew it just as much as the winner did.

The sandbox belonging to Andy Leiblich, the boy next door, is where, the middle-aged narrator remembers, 'I used a toy hoe to kill a boy whose name was Steven Adinoff back in Woodmere when I was six', thereby abbreviating the game, and his childhood:

> I could sit for hours,
> I could go for days.

Constipation, compulsive behaviour, horror of genitalia: Freud beams down fondly on the boy in the sandbox. The narrator of *Dear Mr. Capote* muses over the fluids that emit from the eyes of his victims and considers briefly sticking Paki where he should not, 'Not that you should ever stick a knife in a place like that', yet the very grossness of these reflections turns them, in the context of the novel, into further provocations from an armoury of teases: amazingly, the psychopath as patient. However, the killing in *Peru* perhaps represents a resolution of the anxieties of childhood: when the opportunity arises to define yourself through creating your own primal scene then you grab your toy hoe with both hands.

Quality of life is quality of food: the 6-year-old prepares his own dinner of frankfurters and beans and, puzzled yet envious of Andy Lieblich's diet, questions his mother about broiled meat patties. The Lieblich's home looks good enough to eat, and in dreams he does eat it, savouring the taste of All Sorts. Appetites burgeon and Steven Adinoff is not so much killed as ingested, his face 'like a peach pit with some of the peach still left on it'. As the narrator of *Peru* says:

> I should be skipping the feelings and be sticking to other things, anyway. To what I remember because I actually heard it or saw it or so forth and so on—I should be sticking to things like that before things start getting too mixed up.

This is an odd joke on Lish's part, oddly self-conscious and oddly telling. These are Hemingway's rules for composition, of course, and the speaker ignores them, following his own internal logic. Memory, not machismo, predominates and the rhythms of Lish's prose recall Hemingway's contemporary, Faulkner: too slow or fast, stumbling, stricken. Like Lish's narrator his characters find themselves excluded forever from their non-paradise and, long after euphony has shown the door to sense, manage to scare themselves into telling the truth. Yet lest we should view them as solipsists mired in their own distress, both Lish's narrators warmly introduce themselves as doting fathers, family men. Lish's mass-murderer is offering to sell his memoirs in order to provide for his son's future (he communicates by walkie-talkie whenever they are apart) and the Word-a-Day calendar doubles as educational text and accessory before the fact. In *Peru* the imminent return of his son from summer camp provides a respite from the narrator's recollections; he is also pleased to report that the boy's bowel movements are regular and that he enjoys most of the normal sports. Yet he can't help wondering when reality will begin in earnest: 'I think in theory that he is already strong enough to kill me.'

Dear Mr. Capote may be an inversion of *In Cold Blood*, but it remains conceivable that Capote's novel and *Peru* may bear a similar relation to historical reality. The narrator's parents are Phil and Reg, and his name—again courtesy of the blurb— is 'Gordon'. Denis Donoghue shares the book's dedication with Philip and Regina Lish and 'Steven Michael Adinoff, b. 1934, d. 1940'. This is nothing more than a suggestion, but like much in Lish it is certainly nothing less.

5

The speaker of 'Guilt', the short story that fathers *Peru*, laments that 'I wish I could think of a way to get speech into this without disrupting things. But I don't think I can. If presences could talk, I could do it.' When presences talk in *Peru* it is to draw attention to their talent for silence and their gift for being elegized. ' "Let it never be said, and said to your shame, that all was beauty here before you came." ' The provocative cadences of the Lieblichs' nanny beseech the disaster of fable and folklore, egging on one kind of inevitability. Steven Adinoff embraces quite another, the realization that whatever happens to him must remain

unchecked on the narrative plane yet can be criticized at the
level of conception:

> You want to know what he said?
> You want to hear what Steven Adinoff actually said?
> He said, 'You don't have to kill me.'
> He said, 'You didn't have to kill me.'

Steven Adinoff's literary incarnation views his former
fate with misgivings, a fate that his first remark impossibly
prefigures, since his death is an event not in his but the
speaker's life. The revised version mourns the passing of
the first and shifts the burden of logical impossibility to
the speaking subject. Each constitutes an estrangement of
self from expression: Steven Adinoff cannot make the first
statement and it cannot be Steven Adinoff that is making
the second. The killing that forms the site of remorse in the
narrator's mind is premeditated murder in his victim's. With
the simplicity of a home movie ceaselessly rewinding, Steven
Adinoff spends the novel falling down and staggering up,
grousing about the script and cheerlessly playing his part,
the part of the intelligencer whose message ensures his
despatch. His harelip (' "Nyou nyidn't nyave nyoo nyill
nyee" ') attends 'Gordon's' own social affliction of dispos-
session. He is bad luck incarnate, ominous and ownerless,
unable to attach himself because his handicap precludes
belonging: 'How would you like to be a mother who had to
kiss her boy on a lip like that? There's no choice, there's no
choice.' 'Gordon's' rabid greed for attachment fuels a super-
stitious stress on severance in which logic and its obverse
again feature criminally: 'She wished she could have had
me instead. That way she wouldn't have had to have been
a mother who was glad to have a boy who was dead.'
Peru showers its readership with the *entrées* of several
disciplines, and we might feel equally justified in relating
its central tragedy to Levi-Strauss as to Lacan. However,
Lish's deployment of the killing as a disavowal of the self
in its articulation is consonant with his previous concerns.
The speaker kills to express a self that can no longer exist,
that mutates into its memory: 'I never wanted to be the one
who I am.' It is the confession that is the crime because the

collective force of that memory, the Starchamber thrust of 'You were six', proclaims an immanence that effaces us, that strikes us speechless and shapeless both:

> But there was never anything but just more sand in it. There was never any bug in it. Except it didn't matter the next time, did it? I mean, when you saw another little ball of it that looked like it was going all along all by itself—it was always the terror, wasn't it? And then the murder over and over?
> With nothing ever dead.
> All you ever killed was little clumps of sand.
> No goo ever oozed out, no shell ever cracked, nothing squashed was ever there in your hand—all that was ever in it was just more sand.
> You remember.
> It just took me to show you that you could never forget.

The primal audacity of all this is unanswerable, and suavely pre-empts the reader's propensity to diminish a novel, any novel, to the sum of his own concerns, reabsorbing those concerns to create a new vehicle of expression and a reader without a self. For all that, the trick itself is not new. Proust first wielded this method as a means of subverting the stolidity of the Balzacian novel; in Lish it is extrapolated and tautened to oblige as its own scenario and to give a less gilded refusal of life's possibilities. *Peru* is out of joint with much post-modernist writing in so far as it reorientates its readers, albeit to brand them as a quorum of *misérables*. Its collusiveness contaminates, its intimacy the floodlit fun of the identity parade. If you are not Capote, then you must be Cain.

NOTES

1. *Michigan Quarterly Review*, XXVI, XXVII, 1987–88. For a cross-section of American minimalist fiction see Robert Shapard and James Thomas (eds.), *Sudden Fiction* (Harmondsworth: Penguin, 1988). The anthology contains an uncollected piece by Lish, 'The Merry Chase' (pp. 50–4) and an avuncular *Afterword* (p. 255).
2. Ibid., XXVII, p. 115. Daniel Stern.
3. Ibid., XXVI, p. 711.

4. Gordon Lish was born in New York in 1934 and was fiction editor at *Esquire* from 1969 to 1977. A Lecturer at Columbia University, he received a Guggenheim Fellowship in 1984. His novels are *Dear Mr. Capote* (New York: Holt, Rinehard and Winston, 1983) and *Peru* (New York: E. P. Dutton, 1986). His short story collection *What I Know So Far* appeared in 1984. He is currently senior editor at Alfred A. Knopf and lives in New York. The essay refers to the Sceptre paperback editions of *Dear Mr. Capote* and *Peru* and the 1986 Scribner Signature edition of *What I Know So Far*.
5. Ian Hamilton, *In Search of J. D. Salinger* (London: William Heinemann, 1988), p. 198.
6. Gerald Clarke, *Capote* (London: Hamish Hamilton, 1988), pp. 318–47.
7. Ibid., p. 346.
8. Ibid., p. 344.
9. Ibid., p. 327.
10. Ibid., pp. 461–73, 483–94.
11. Norman Mailer, *Advertisements for Myself* (London: Panther Books, 1968) pp. 380–81.
12. Clarke, p. 471.
13. Ibid., p. 326.
14. Ibid., p. 461.
15. Hamilton, op. cit., Arnold Goldman, *The Lives of John Lennon* (London: Transworld, 1988).

6

Ethnic Renaissance: Rudolfo Anaya, Louise Erdrich and Maxine Hong Kingston

by A. ROBERT LEE

> Ethnic art *is* the American mainstream. . . .
> —Ishmael Reed, Interview, 'The Third Ear', B.B.C.
> Radio 3, April 1989[1]
>
> Growing up ethnic is surely the liveliest theme to appear in
> the American novel since the closing of the frontier. . . .
> —John Skow, reviewing Amy Tan, *The Joy Luck Club*,
> *Time*, 27 March 1989[2]

1

A vogue it may currently appear. But can it be doubted
that ethnicity has ever been other than a key ingredient in
American culture? One thinks of founding racial encounters:
Columbus sighting his 'gentle' Arawak Indians in the 1490s
and they him, Cortés imposing Spanish imperial rule upon
Aztec Mexico and the American southwest after arriving
at Mexico City in 1519, or those first twenty enslaved
Africans being deposited in Jamestown in 1619 from a
reputed Dutch man-of-war.[3] One thinks, subsequently, of
the great ensuing waves of European immigration, each the
bearer of a culture in its own right yet each to be made over

into a new hyphenation with America—Anglos, Irish, Scots, Germans, Slavs, Italians, Scandinavians, Jews out of Russia and Poland. To these has to be added the Asian diaspora, from the early Chinese who spoke of San Francisco as 'The Gold Mountain' to the Japanese to the latter-day Korean and Vietnamese. The process in no way abates.

There would emerge, too, a now familiar body of ethnic debate. Was America melting-pot or mixing bowl, a W.A.S.P. hegemony or a genuine quilt of all peoples?[4] Yet however long-standing or endemic the issue of ethnicity in America, it was in the 1960s as never before that it took on new prominence, new assertion. For during that turbulent decade and thereafter ethnic America, and above all non-European ethnic America, re-announced itself. The process was political, economic, a bid for long-overdue empowerment. It was also cultural, a major and continuing surge of imaginative self-expression.

To cite the 1960s from an ethnic or racial perspective of necessity first means a reference-back to the call for redress by black America. No clearer index of change offered itself than the use of Black for Negro, the latter discarded as belonging to a time about to pass and to a more traditional and quiescent racial equation. Other changes, however, were nothing if not dramatic—the Civil Rights marches, the push for voter registration in the Dixie South, the long hot summers, the city burnings from New Jersey to Watts and from Atlanta to Detroit, and the emergence of Black Power groups like the Panthers and Muslims. Tragically, too, there was the litany of assassinations, whether Jack and Bobby Kennedy, or Medgar Evers, or Martin Luther King, or Malcolm X, or George Jackson. Yet as the legislation got on the books, as a pantheon of new black leadership emerged, and as the American media increasingly took note of its black population, few doubted that an end to any supposed one-standard America lay in prospect.

Artists, film-makers, musicians, journalists, sports stars and comics all played their part, supplying fresh codes and images of American blackness. Literary figures, in especial, contributed. A fiction begun in names like those of Ralph Ellison and James Baldwin has continued through into the generation of Ishmael Reed, James Alan McPherson and even beyond. A line of writing by Afro-American women has come to prominence, Ann Petry and Paule Marshall from an earlier time and Toni Morrison, Alice Walker and Gayl Jones from among their successors. New departures in poetry, theatre and film have made their impact, as has a rich vein of autobiographical work stretching from Malcolm X to LeRoi Jones/Amiri Baraka and from Eldridge Cleaver to Maya Angelou. Then, too, there was the galvanizing effect of Alex Haley's *Roots* (1976), both the novel and the spectacularly widely viewed T.V. series. Whether 'Black' truly had become 'Beautiful' as the slogan ran, it had without a doubt called time on past assumptions. Not without cause has there been talk of a Second Renaissance of Afro-American art and ideas.[5]

But central as was this black efflorescence, it tended to eclipse others. Hispanic or Brown America lay in waiting, demographically the largest impending minority in America: Puerto Ricans in New York, *emigré* Cubans in Florida, Chileans, Salvadoreans, Argentinians and others in flight from dictatorship, and, above all, Mexican-Americans or Chicanos. These latter not only arose out of a profoundly non-Anglo tradition—Aztec-Spanish, Catholic, border Mexican—but out of their own variety of American Spanish and bilingualism. Theirs, too, was another geography, California, Texas, Arizona, New Mexico, Colorado and southern Utah, not to mention another set of cultural styles from foodways to low-rider cars. Equally, they could look back upon their own interpretation of history, be it the Mexican–American War (1846–48), Mexican Independence (1910), the Sleepy Lagoon and Zoot Suit Riots (1943), or the continuing influx across the Rio Grande. The 1960s meant César Chávez and the struggle of his U.F.W. (founded in 1962) to fight the grape-picking wars. They also meant Corky González and the Denver Crusade for Justice and José Angel Gutiérrez and La Raza Unida of Texas. They even came to mean the increasing recognition of a Chicano input into general American usage—*Aztlán* as the mythical homeland of the Chicano people and words like *la raza* (literally 'the race'), *mestizo* (someone of mixed Indian and Spanish blood) and *pachuco* (young male Chicano). In literary-cultural terms they also meant nothing less than a Chicano Renaissance: Luis Valdez's *Teatro Campesino*, or the fiction of Tomás Rivera, Rudolfo Anaya, Ron Arias and others, or the poetry of Alurista and Bernice Zamora, or Richard Rodriguez's controversial autobiography *Hunger of Memory* (1982). Thus as *The Milagro Beanfield War*, *East LA* and *Stand and Deliver* win out in their depictions of Chicano life on American cinema screens, there can be little doubt that *Chicanismo*, too, has established new rights to attention.[6]

Blacks and Chicanos were to find their counterparts among the Indians of America. Reservation-based or urban, they in their turn felt moved to call time on their past demoralization. Typical was the replacement of the name 'Indian' itself with 'Native-American', another break with white nomenclature. Typical, too, were events like the challenge of the National Indian Youth Council and the American Indian Movement (A.I.M., founded in 1969) to the traditional powers of the Bureau of Indian Affairs; or the occupations and land claims in Alcatraz, Taos, Maine and Massachusetts; or the seizure in 1973 by Sioux activists of the historic village of Wounded Knee in the Pine Ridge Reservation of South Dakota; or the emergence of a militant new generation of leaders like Dennis Banks and Russell Means. To hand, also, were manifestos and re-interpretations like Vine Deloria's *Custer Died for your Sins* (1969) and *Behind the Trail of Broken Treatises* (1974). Non-Indian scholarship likewise took up the call, none more so than Leslie Fiedler's *The Return of the Vanishing American* (1968), an analysis of the hidden 'Red America' within both high and popular American culture, and Dee Brown's *Bury my Heart at Wounded Knee* (1970), a history which examines the brutal cost to the Indian of the Winning of the West with its white triumphalist myth of frontier and settlement.[7] Brown took as his departure-point the 'graves of the dead' as the Shawnee chief, Tecumseh, once put it. All of this was to have its literary manifestation, nothing less than another genuine contemporary American renaissance. In quick order appeared fiction like: *House Made of Dawn* (1968) by the Kiowa, N. Scott Momaday; *Seven Arrows* (1972) by the Cheyenne, Heyemeyohsts Storm;

Winter in the Blood (1974) by the Blackfoot, James Welch; *Ceremony* (1978) by the Laguna, Leslie Marmon Silko; and, to be sure, the Chippewa-inspired story-telling of Louise Erdrich. To these has to be added the poetry of talent like Gerald Vizenor, Simon Ortiz, Gail Tremblay and Joy Harjo. Once again, a new ethnic and cultural contract was being sought with America.[8]

Asian-Americans were to have their day slightly later, in the 1980s. Theirs, too, like 'Hispanic' has been a composite name, in need of clear particularization into Chinese-American, Japanese-American and the like.[9] America's Chinese have had to fight off a more than usually entrenched set of popular-culture stereotypes, those of coolie, cook and launderer. Sax Rohmer's Fu Manchu and Earl Derr Biggers's Charlie Chan respectively bequeathed greatly influential images of 'bad' and 'good' Chinese, as likewise did Chop-Chop in the massively popular cartoon series *Blackhawk* (1941–84).[10] Against these odds and the daemonology of 'Red China', a new and largely West Coast flowering has been under way. So, at least, would be the evidence of the memoir work of Maxine Hong Kingston (her first novel, *Tripmaster Monkey*, is currently announced), the drama of Frank Chin—especially *The Chickencoop Chinamen* (1972) and *The Year of The Dragon* (1974)—and novels like *Homebase* (1979) by Shawn Wong, *Thousand Pieces of Gold* (1981) by Ruthanne Lum McCunne, and latterly, *The Joy Luck Club* (1989) by Amy Tan. Similarly Japanese-Americans have had to contend against the inherited stigmas of Pearl Harbour, the Pacific islands wars, and their removal to Californian and other 'relocation' camps during World War II. That story, and more, has been told by the likes of Monica Sone, Hisaye Yamamoto and Toshio Mori. Furthermore, the Asian-American literary roster grows, as can be witnessed in the ongoing fiction and essays of the Filipino-American, Carlos Bulosan (*America is in the Heart* (1946, 1973) as notably as any), or in a novel like *Clay Walls* (1986) by the Korean-American, Kim Ronyoung, or in *Blue Dragon White Tiger* (1978) by the Vietnamese-American, Tran Van Dinh.[11] *Time* magazine, even if its focus was business and yuppiedom rather than culture, did no more than mirror another ethnic cycle of change

143

when it gave over a whole issue in mid-1988 to Asian America.[12]

Anaya, Erdrich, Kingston: these three names, then, must do composite duty. They have every cause to be taken wholly on their own terms, powerful imaginations each. Yet as, respectively, Chicano, Native-American and Chinese-American, they also have drawn profoundly and quite inescapably from their different ethnic legacies. In each case, too, they have lived both within and yet at an angle from what passes as 'mainstream' America, a truly hyphenated or joint cultural citizenry as it were. In imagining 'ethnically', thereby, they offer the paradox of having written into being an America the nation barely knew itself to be, another and yet the same America.

2

A historic first presence in the American southwest, a landscape as much of custom and language as of place, and the interplay of an ancestral Aztec legacy with a missionary-derived Catholicism—it hardly surprises that Chicano fiction has been so taken up with its communal past. Few Chicanos, writers or otherwise, have not pondered their pre-Columbian origins (for the most part it is carried in their facial appearance and skin colour), or the antiquity of their own legends and religion, or the push westwards and north into a supposed Yankee El Dorado. That consciousness, certainly, has pressed hard behind the landmarks of the achievement, novels like José Antonio Villarreal's *Pocho* (1959), generally acknowledged as the first Chicano novel and which portrays the Rubio family's bitter migration into California, or John Rechy's *City of Night* (1963), in line with his other fiction essentially a novel of homosexual transience but which also reflects his early Chicano and Texas origins, or Tomás Rivera's *. . . y no se lo tragó la tierra* (*. . . and the earth did not part*, 1970), a story-cycle set in Texas and unfolded through the persona of an unnamed child as a conflict of Chicano and Anglo cultures (rightly it has been compared with Joyce's *Dubliners* and Anderson's *Winesburg, Ohio*), or, of late, Ron Arias's *The Road To Tamazunchale* (1987), a fantastical dream novel told as the last words of Don Fausto, a dying Chicano elder who looks back from the Los Angeles *barrio* upon his community's meaning and inheritance.[13] To these has to be added a body of *literatura chicanesca*, writing about Chicano life by non-Chicanos, of which indisputably the foremost since the Robert Redford film version has been John Nichols's *The Milagro Beanfield War* (1976)—the first in a New Mexico trilogy.[14]

Within this frame, Rudolfo Anaya has equally laid down his own terms of reference and nowhere more so than in the novel which continues most to secure his reputation, *Bless Me, Ultima* (1972).[15] Set in the rural New Mexico of World War II, it tells the rite of passage of 8-year-old Antonio Márez—Tony as he will become with anglicization—an evocation by turns tender and fierce of a unique Chicano childhood. For into its telling, Anaya brilliantly imports a whole stock of dynastic history, myth and belief, that of a people caught at the turning-point between a Mexican-hispanic past and an American-hispanic future. Presiding over the whole is the shamanistic figure of Ultima, known also as La Grande, a *curandera* or healer-sage under whose guiding kindliness Antonio falls. An inspired fusion of eventfulness and dream, the historic and the ceremonial, *Bless Me, Ultima* also yields its own Portrait of the Artist, the boy's emerging measure of his inheritance subtly rewoven into a first-person work of memory. Anaya's subsequent two novels, *Heart of Aztlán* (1976) and *Tortuga* (1979), the former which deals with the transition of a rural family into the urban *barrio* of Barelas in Albuquerque and the latter with the path into recovery and self-independence of a crippled boy (*tortuga*, tortoise, refers to his hospital plaster cast), may indeed represent a certain drop in power. But they share with *Bless Me, Ultima*, which deservedly won the prestigious Second Annual Premio Quinto Sol, a belief in the as yet still untold reaches of Chicano life.

'Every morning I seem to awaken with a new experience and dreams strangely mixed in me.' So Antonio looks back on his self-proclaimed 'magical' New Mexico upbringing, caught as he is between the Márez legacy of his father, one of *vaquero* or herdsman life on the *llano* (flatlands), and the Luna legacy of his mother, one of homestanding and cultivation of the land. Márez as against Luna might also be said to signify male and female principles, *conquistador* as against settler and homemaker. If, too, Gabriel hopes his son will reincarnate a nomadic past glory, his wife hopes the boy will become a priest and farmer like one of her own first ancestors. For *Bless Me, Ultima* portrays nothing if not worlds in transition. Gabriel Márez has moved in from the *llano* to the *pueblo*, works not with horses and cattle but in a highway repair crew, and if he looks backwards to the myth of his ancestors he also seeks to look forwards to his family's eventual (though unlikely) migration to California. A larger frame is also provided by the reference to the Second World War. Nearby lies Los Alamos (The Poplars), the testing site for the first atomic bomb and the instance of a technology at quite the other end of the time spectrum to that which has produced the Márez and Luna clans. Transition, too, is registered in the enlistment of Antonio's three brothers, eventual returnee GIs who come from battles in Japan and Germany not to stay but to become drifters seeking an easy pleasure in Las Vegas (The Lowlands). Aztec, Mexican or New Mexican as may be the sub-stratum of Antonio's land and history, yet, too, another transition pends—that brought on by his beginning studies of English, the pull of Yankee America for his cultural allegiance.

The novel's essential transitions, however, occur in terms of the boy himself, 'experience' and 'dream' indeed 'strangely mixed'. In the former column, Anaya has Antonio witness the arrival in the family home of Ultima, his father's story-telling and drinking, intervals working the land with his mother's relatives at El Puerto, his first schooling, and the tugs and tensions of early boyhood friendship. He also witnesses four dramatically told deaths: that of Lupito, a war-veteran mentally damaged in Japan who shoots Chávez, the sheriff, and who typifies a madness imported from 'the outside'; that of Narciso, the town's basically harmless drunk killed by Tenorio Trementina who believe Ultima a *bruja* or witch responsible for the death of one of his daughters but for whom Narciso has only gratitude and love; that of Florence, a boy who drowns and with whom Antonio has

struck up a bond of private sympathy and ritual; and that of
Ultima herself, who teaches him that death can be continuity
and restoration as well as separation. He also undergoes a
cycle of childhood fevers and acts of witness as when he
sees the Lupito killing or is assailed by an avenging Tenorio
astride his horse or sees Ultima cure with secret herbs a
member of the Téllez family. Yet, wonderfully conceived
and patterned as these events are, they in effect serve as
supports to even deeper transitions taking place within
Antonio Márez's inward being.

In these, dream and myth play key rôles, most of all in
connection with Ultima. Antonio dreams of his own birth
and *'the old woman'* who delivered him (*'Only I will know
his destiny'*, Ultima announces); he dreams several times of
his three brothers, fugitive elder presences who strike out in
directions he slowly realizes he cannot follow; he dreams of
Tenorio's dead daughter (*'my dream-fate drew me to the coffin'*),
a vision with Macbethian overtones of witchery and magic;
and, above all, he dreams of the legend of the Golden Carp, a
huge fish which swims about the waters flowing beneath and
about his *pueblo* and which is protected and half-worshipped
by his friends Samuel and Cisco. The carp exists in fact and
fantasy, a literal river fish but also a source of legend. Samuel
explains how, in communal myth, the carp incarnates a
protector-god, the deity of land and people:

> . . . he went to the other gods and told them that he chose to
> be turned into a carp and swim in the river where he could take
> good care of his people. The gods agreed. But because he was a
> god they made him very big and colored him the color of gold.
> And they made him the lord of all the waters of the valley.

The carp, thus, mediates a world of fact and superstition,
actuality and dream. And, for Antonio, it also supplies a
counter to the Catholicism in which Father Byrne and the
church have begun giving him instruction. A dilemma thus
arises for the boy: which offers the better theology, an Indian
animism or the Christianity of the Easter Week against which
are set the later parts of the novel? Whichever Antonio's
choice, both now co-exist as resources in the boy's nascent
creative psyche.

So, too, and in overwhelming fashion, does Ultima. No obscure peyote or psychedelic cultist out of Carlos Castaneda, she is truly *una última*, one of the last of an ancient order. A Catholic believer, she nonetheless incarnates a oneness with prior and non-Christian stores of knowledge, the spirituality of the natural order. Not that Anaya turns her into mere formula or symbol; far from it. He depicts her as a credibly live presence, a bearer of the past but also for Antonio at least a major figure of his present. More still to the point, perhaps, she will be a crucial remembered presence in his future. From the start, too, he understands the meaning of the owl as her titular emblem ('with Ultima came the owl'), a totem whose every successive cry heralds a major turn not only in her life but his own. It is the owl which attacks Tenorio in his first attempt to destroy Ultima and puts out his eye; the owl which accompanies her on her every mission; and the owl which when finally killed by Tenorio signals also her own inevitable death. Antonio acts both as her apprentice and her memorialist. She so in addition calls out his rising creative-imaginative sympathies, his artist's ability to see *curandera* and owl at once literally and figuratively yet without the slightest undue contradiction.

No account of *Bless Me, Ultima*, too, can pass over lightly Anaya's passionate sense of New Mexico not simply as region or place but as a storehouse of past Chicano identity. He himself has spoken of its hold for him in interview:

> [The] landscape plays a major rôle in the literature that I write. In the beginning, it is an empty, desolate, bare stage; then, if one looks closely, one sees life—people gather to tell stories, to do their work, to love, to die. In the old days the sheep and cattle ranchers gathered in that small village, which had a train station, watering station for the old coal-burning trains. It was prosperous; they were good times. Then after the visit or the business at hand is done, the people disappear back into the landscape and you're left as if alone, with the memories, dreams, stories, and whatever joys and tragedies they have brought to you.[16]

Bless Me, Ultima clearly arose out of this store of 'memories, dreams [and] stories', a triumph both for what they so

palpably have given to him but which by the same token he
has given back to them.

3

As typically 'Indian' a moment as any in Louise Erdrich's
three novels—in sequence *Love Medicine* (1984), *The Beet
Queen* (1986) and *Tracks* (1988)—occurs in *The Beet Queen*
when Russell Kashpaw, a Chippewa from North Dakota and
a Korean war veteran, is honoured by his state as its 'most
decorated hero'.[17] In fact Russell has been shot to pieces,
become an alcoholic, and needs a wheelchair after suffering
a stroke. As the celebrants mill about him, he has a vision of
sorts in which he sees himself as already dead and in which
he calls to mind his Chippewa background:

> . . . this was the road that old-time Chippewas talked about,
> the four-day road of death. He'd just started out.
> I'm dead now, he thought with calm wonder.
> At first he was sorry that it had happened in public, instead
> of some private place. Then he was glad, and he was also
> glad to see that he hadn't lost his sense of humor even now.
> It struck him as so funny that the town he'd lived in and the
> members of the American Legion were solemnly saluting a
> dead Indian, that he started to shake with laughter.

In evidence, here, are a number of Erdrich hallmarks: her
sense of Indian history as a mix of defeat and victory,
her use of the 'four-day road' as indicative of a wholly
unique Chippewa-Indian cosmology and way of being, her
well-taken smack at stereotype ('The only good Indian . . .'
etc.), and her resort to an irony which can envisage the
transformation of a maimed latter-day Indian warrior into
an all-American super-patriot. She also plays into Russell's
musings a tough laconicism, an idiom sharply his own
and at once inward yet free of contrivance or simple self-
pity. In building her Chippewa world Erdrich barely misses
a step, and not least besides these kinds of feature by
supplying an insider's backdrop of North Dakota and the
American–Canadian border. Her Indian 'mythical kingdom'
may, as it further evolves, come to be thought of a kind
with Faulkner's Yoknapatawpha (not irrelevantly itself a

Chickasaw-Indian name) or that, say, of Flannery O'Connor's hardshell Georgia.

Nor, for Erdrich, has 'Indian' meant only mere *donnée* or theme. Figuratively speaking an 'Indian' pattern runs right through her novels, one in which the circle is all and life operates as a kind of mysterious or magic revolving wheel. Her story-logic so foregoes linear development. Characters, mainly indeed from Chippewa dynasties like the Kashpaws and the Lamartines, touch, move on, intermarry and feud, all of them contributing human spokes in the turning order of things. It takes a while always to get steady bearings in this kind of fiction, though no more so than in much of Faulkner or Joyce. Each of the three novels, accordingly, offers stories (often enough monologues) complete in themselves yet at the same time circularly webbed one into the other. Erdrich moves in this way back and forth through both space and time—in one perspective Argus, North Dakota, and its surrounding reservations and 'allotments', and in another, Chippewa history from the turn of the century down into the 1980s. She genuinely both startles and compels, wholly deserving of Philip Roth's accolade as 'the most interesting new novelist to have appeared in years'.[18]

Love Medicine, fourteen linked pieces in all, inaugurates the Chippewa Kashpaw-Lamartine cycle. In 'The World's Greatest Fishermen', the first story, a Chippewa woman, June Kashpaw, wills her own death by walking into the night-time snows outside of Williston, North Dakota ('a town full of rich, single cowboy-rigger oil trash'). Her death, as indeed her life of missed chances, throws a forward shadow over the events subsequently unfolded. Thereafter, too, we meet other Kashpaws and Lamartines, together with the Lazarres, the Pillagers, the Morrisseys, the Nanapushes and the Adares—Indians, 'mixed' and non-Indians each severally bound up in the one communal hoop. Families vie for the ever-reducing tribal land. Odd couplings and liaisons and births take place. White as against red values clash. The stories deal, too, with the tensions between a French-exported Catholicism and Chippewa belief ('Saint Marie' and 'Flesh and Blood'), the unexpected turns of Indian conjure and potions ('Love Medicine'), the rôle of drink and alcoholism in Chippewa history ('Crown of Thorns'), sexual permutations within an Indian extended family régime ('Lulu's Boys'), Vietnam and the return of a damaged Henry Lamartine ('The Red Convertible'), and actual tribal reality in an era of mythified or cartoon Indians ('The Plunge of the Brave').[19] Yet as serious in implication as these themes evidently are, Erdrich again keeps them free of solemnity or sentimentalism by the sheer dexterity of her story-telling voice. Narrators accordingly settle old scores, adjust the record as fits, complain or justify, only to have correctives supplied by others in the wheel. Lulu Lamartine in 'The Good Tears' offers a key instance. 'I'm going to tell you about the men', she announces. In short order we learn about Nector Kashpaw, the 'rifraff Morrissey' and the brothers Henry and Bev Lamartine, a black comedy of revolving marriages and relationships. But whatever she grainily discloses about these aspects of her life, her voice is also caught in the following typical aside:

> All through my life I never did believe in human measurement. Numbers, time, inches, feet. All are just ploys for cutting nature down to size. I know the grand scheme of the world is beyond our brains to fathom, so I don't try, just let it in. I don't believe in numbering God's creatures. I never let the United States census in my door, even though they say it's good for Indians. Well, quote me. I say that every time they counted us they knew the precise number to get rid of.

Not only does this put us in the presence of a marvellously singular woman, but of a history, a human bedrock of experience, which reaches out to Chippewa and Indian lives well beyond her own. Erdrich's feat is to make the one idiom precisely imply others.

The Beet Queen, at first sight, would seem a slightly less Indian-centred narrative, which is anything but to say the Kashpaws and their kin do not make frequent appearances. But the novel's 'Indianness' again equally lies elsewhere, in Erdrich's resort to her own highly particular kind of narrative. Wheel, hoop or circle the story turns and turns again, yet never out of control or as mere authorial pyrotechnics. Told across a thirty-year span and again through linking first-person voices, it opens with Mary and Karl Adare, 11 and 14 respectively in 1932, who arrive illicitly by boxcar in Argus, North Dakota, to claim kin with Fritzie and Pete, their aunt and uncle and the owners of Kozka's Meats. Their mother, Adelaide, recently widowed and nothing if not crazy for romance, has dumped not only them but a new-born baby brother to fly south from Minnesota to Florida with 'The Great Omar', a none-too-successful aviator stuntman. At Argus, the two Adare children are separated. Karl, alarmed by a fierce dog, jumps back on the train only to find himself in the amorous clinch of a hobo who rejoices in the name of Giles Saint Ambrose. Despite believing he has found love, Karl now does plunge out of the train, only to break both his legs and be nursed back to health by the journeying Fleur Pillager, Chippewa medicine-woman. Subsequently raised in a Catholic orphanage, he then takes to the road as a salesman of farm and household gadgetry. Mary, meantime, goes about the wheel of her life somewhat differently. Her girlhood she spends in fierce tension with her disturbed, glamour-struck cousin Sita. She even becomes the centre of what Argus dubs a religious miracle. And in due course, a spinsterish Annie Oakley figure and purveyor of beef and pork, she takes over the meat business.

The lives of the two Adares, however, are but two spokes in the wheel. Clementine James, part-Indian and Mary's lifelong friend, allows Karl to father a child on her, whom Mary virtually adopts and promptly names Dot. But Dot's actual given name is Wallacene. This links us to Wallace Pfeff, also Dot's self-appointed guardian and the bachelor President of the Argus Chamber of Commerce. Wallace is the man responsible for introducing sugar beet into the region as a sure-fire cash crop. His life, in turn, circles into that of Karl Adare. For he has to live with a lonely secret. The only experience which in any way transforms an otherwise stale round of Babbittry is his darkly comic sexual encounter with Mary's driven but seductive brother. Clementine, too, contributes her brother to the ongoing circle, namely Russell Kashpaw, an Indian as noted both dead and alive. He, more than anyone, can see his enclosure in the Indian wheel.

But it is to Dot that the novel finally reverts, with further linking turns into the lives of Adelaide, Sita, the lost Adare who surfaces as Father Miller, a Catholic priest, the Kashpaw family and others. As Wallace Pfeff intends it, Dot will be the Queen in Argus's Sugar Beet Festival. But there again the wheel turns unexpectedly. She sees that things have been rigged in her favour, gives way to a fury of her own, and like her grandmother Adelaide before her, takes to the skies. That is, she soars off with the local sky-writing pilot only to wheel back to earth when the main events of the festival are over.

One vital clue to the links which bring together all these lives resides in an observation made by Clementine James as she watches a small white spider busy about its labours: 'A web was forming, a complicated house.' Louise Erdrich could not have spoken better of her own finely spun novel. This is a tale bordering on magic—magic history, however, rather than magic realism. It captures the oddness of lives touching unexpectedly, though actually being organized by that very self-same unexpectedness. *The Beet Queen* yields an Indian story indeed, one whose 'Chippewa' logic invites and deserves our keenest recognition.

Tracks steps back an increment in time, to the years 1912–24, and tells of the double-jeopardy suffered by the Chippewa from pneumonia and the loss of tribal lands to outside speculators. Two voices preside, those of old Nanapush, Chippewa tribal Chairman, and of Pauline Lamartine, would-be Catholic martyr, who despite her every effort to break free of her Chippewa allegiances finds herself hexed and drawn back into her Indian heritage. A third, and crucial, point of reference is once again Fleur Pillager, to many of her tribes-people a witch yet to those who know better a lover and intimate. To her daughter, Lulu Pillager, she offers a special female testimony and wisdom, more than anything given her detractors the example of her own self-acceptance. Nanapush for his part speaks out of the past, looking back to a time when 'it would have taken four days to walk the length of this reservation.' Yet he, too, harbours a usable wisdom for the future. 'Nanapush is a name', he declares, 'that loses power every time that it is written and stored in a government file.' Pauline's furious attempts to divest herself of her Indian identity thus makes a wonderfully ironic point of contrast. Between them, as Erdrich shows in each alternating act of witness, they also tell the other and even more important story of the miracle of how the Chippewas have managed to endure.

Like its predecessors, *Tracks* does not always afford too easy or immediate an access, but it continues to exhibit its author's mastery of narrative as a gallery or round of evidentiary voices. The history, too, to which these voices speak and of which in fact they are a part, may well deal in bitterest loss, fissure or simple survival, but not at the expense of any drop in imaginative freshness or vigour on Erdrich's part. Nowhere does the novel show this more typically and affectingly than in the account given by Pauline Lamartine of a prophetic earlier moment in the life of Nanapush:

> As a young man, he had guided a buffalo expedition for whites. He said the animals understood what was happening, how they were dwindling. He said that when the smoke cleared and hulks lay scattered everywhere, a day's worth of shooting for only the tongues and hides, the beasts that survived grew strange and unusual. They lost their minds. They bucked, screamed and stamped, tossed the carcasses and grazed on flesh. They tried their best to cripple one another, to fall or die. They tried suicide. They tried to do away with their young. They knew they were going, saw their end. He said while the whites all slept through the terrible night he kept watch, that the groaning never stopped, that the plain below him was alive, a sea turned against itself, and when the thunder came, then and only then, did the madness cease. He saw their spirits slip between the lightning sheets.

As its title implies, *Tracks* seeks to develop both a wholly specific Chippewa story and at the same time a still larger historic story of the kind which lies parabolically inscribed within this recollection. Louise Erdrich's imaginative feat is to draw us into both stories in equal part. Indian—Native-American—fiction has rarely been better served.

4

As Maxine Hong Kingston vividly attests in *The Woman Warrior: Memoirs of a Childhood Among Ghosts* (1977) and *China Men* (1980), few ethnic hyphenations can have involved more by way of a juncture of opposites than Chinese-American.[20] Who, better than she, certainly, has brought more informed or passionate witness to bear in dramatizing the play of the two regimes: a China whose ideograph signifies the centre of the world, whose ancestors require daily assuagement and worship, and for whom the past in every way determines the present; and an America now become the new imperium, whose worship (at least under a Californian dispensation) is of a gratificatory here and now, and where pastness if not exactly abolished is to be pushed down and back? Nor, for Kingston, do the disjunctures stop there. Yellow-white gaps abound, be it in language, the relation of space to time, ritual, the status of family or women or children, the nature of eating, or even the loudness of talk. Both books explore with quite simple brilliance the configuration of a diasporaized Han people (Mandarin, Cantonese or whichever) who not only live among their own ghosts but among 'foreign devil' ghost-people, the non-Chinese, of America. For Kingston, born and raised (perhaps inevitably in a laundry) at the Californian turning-point between these opposite and frequently opposed worlds, an East and a West, an Old and a New, the paradoxes of her birthright from childhood onwards have as she insists virtually pressed for articulation, an obligatory telling. Her two volumes, paired compendia of autobiography, myth, essay and history made over into unified narrative, do every justice.

The prospectus she sets up in *The Woman Warrior* begins understandably on a note of interrogation:

> Those of us in the first American generations have had to figure out how the invisible world the emigrants built around our childhoods fit in solid America.
> The emigrants confused the gods by diverting their curses, misleading them with crooked streets and false names. They must try to confuse their offspring as well, who, I suppose, threaten them in similar ways—always trying to get things

straight, always trying to name the unspeakable. The Chinese I know hide their names; sojourners take new names when their lives change and guard their real names with silence.

Chinese-Americans, when you try to understand what things in you are Chinese, how do you separate what is peculiar to childhood, to poverty, insanities, one family, your mother who marked your growing with stories, from what is Chinese? What is Chinese tradition and what is the movies?

Hidden indeed applies. Kingston's rôle is one of excavation, 'figuring out'—of China as first source, of Chineseness in America, of who and what she is herself. This latter involves not only history and ethnicity, however, but gender. For she sees herself in the image of her 'drowned-in-the-well' aunt, that of the creative-autonomous or 'warrior' woman of her book's title.

Told as a five-acter, *The Woman Warrior* negotiates in lavish detail past and present, there and here, the spaces both within and outside Kingston as the operating 'I' of the story. The opening sequence, 'No Name Woman', deals with 'my aunt, my forerunner', a woman who, in having plotted her own sexual destiny, had a child, been hounded to death by her Chinese village as an adulteress and shaming disrupter of the established order, in revenge drowns herself in the communal drinking water. She thereby becomes one of the most powerful of ghosts in the Chinese firmament, a water ghost. She also, decades later, comes to 'haunt' her niece, a Chinese woman-relation and exemplar of undefeated (though not unpunished) strength. Outlaw, pioneer, warrior, in naming her thus Kingston equally names the self she, too, would like to be. The sequence which then follows, 'White Tigers', tells the complementary myth of My Lan, a swordswoman warrior and 'female avenger' who rids her land of foreign usurpation. She, like the aunt, serves as a presence Kingston hopes to incorporate into herself ('I would have to grow up a warrior woman'). But so resolved, and in a nice time switch to the 1960s as America's supposedly most liberated decade, Kingston realizes that the old curbs and dispensations still cling: 'I went away to college—Berkeley in the sixties—and I studied, and I marched to change the world, but I did not turn into a boy. . . .' She even speaks with some envy of

Japanese immigrants who can find unchanging rôle models in the samurai and geishas. For her, living among American ghosts as her parents designate them, she must find new ways of being a swordswoman. She must, as it were, remake her Chineseness, neither quite that of China nor quite that of America but a Chineseness of her own making and which can adapt and reshape as necessary. To do that, too, she has no option but to combat the racism and ignorance which surround her, 'the nigger yellow' attributed to her by one employer and the dehumanizations implied in language like 'gook' and 'chink'.

'Shaman' calls up her mother's life as a trained midwife in China, especially the memory of her medical certificate ('When I open it, the smell of China flies out . . .'). She looks back to how her mother, Brave Orchid, became for her village patients not only a trafficker in pills and bandages but also a magician, an exorcist of bad ghosts. 'The students at the Keung School of Midwifery', Kingston recalls, 'were new women, scientists who changed the rituals.' On leaving China in 1939 with the Japanese invasion only recently behind her, Brave Orchid would find new ghosts to have to confront, an America full of 'Taxi Ghosts', 'Bus Ghosts', 'Police Ghosts', and, some years later, 'Urban Renewal Ghosts'. Americans, she comes to think, are all 'work ghosts', with 'no time for acrobatics'. Her life, like that of her daughter after her, becomes that of the laundry, and with the original village land in China sold she has 'no more China to go home to'. Whatever thus ensues, it will have to ensue in America, Brave Orchid as both emigrant and immigrant, and Kingston in her wake as the 'author' both of her mother's story and her own. In 'At the Western Palace' the perspective broadens to include the saga of Brave Orchid's sister, Moon Orchid, who at the age of 68 and having travelled through Hong Kong, brings still more 'business begun in China' into Kingston's life. Having waited nearly fifteen years Moon Orchid seeks her long-emigrated and now re-married husband ('He looked and smelled like an American'), begins to deteriorate mentally under the stress of her husband's repudiation and her own foreignness (she 'misplaces herself in space' as Brave Orchid calls it), and ends up in an all-woman asylum deludedly but contentedly believing on the grounds that they never depart that her fellow inmates are none other than her own 'daughters'. Two worlds have this time met but not fused, a species of disjuncture contemplated more than a little ruefully by Kingston.

'A Song for a Barbarian Reed', which rounds out the volume, begins with Brave Orchid cutting her daughter's tongue 'so that you would not be tongue-tied', an unerring prophetic act for the writer and feminist her daughter would become. The girl, so released, grows up among a world of ethnic diversity ('I liked the Negro students (Black Ghosts) best because they talked the loudest and talked to me because I was a daring talker too'). Selfhood, too, turns into an issue in the very calligraphy of English:

> I could not understand 'I.' The Chinese 'I' has seven strokes, intricacies. How could the American 'I,' assuredly wearing a hat like the Chinese, have only three strokes, the middle so straight?

She ponders, relatedly, the auditary impression of Chinese speech on English-only Americans and American speech on Chinese-only immigrants. To American ears she thinks Chinese sounds 'chingchong ugly', whereas in reverse 'the Chinese can't hear American at all; the language is too soft.' Other fissures equally trouble her: between being as she calls it 'Chinese-feminine' and 'American-feminine' ('American-Chinese girls have to whisper to make ourselves American-feminine'); between the general openness of manner of Americans and 'the secrecy of the Chinese' (' "Don't tell," said my parents'); and between the 'vampire nightmares' of her Chinese past and the matching fear of becoming 'the crazy one' of her American present. But, over time, the talker and writer and trickster in her grows to the point where she knows she 'can do ghost things even better than ghosts can'. Appropriately, the final myth she alludes to has to do with the 'song' of Ts'ai Yen, a second-century poetess, who was captured by barbarians, had two children by the chieftain neither of whom grew up speaking Chinese, and who learned that the barbarians's 'reed music' about 'for ever wandering' she must learn to attend to and respect as much as her own original culture. The fable bears utterly on the relation of ancestral China with the Chinese-Americans who have come to live within reach of 'The Gold Mountain', an Asian world yet at the same time and in every way as deservingly an American world. It makes the perfect coda to the odyssey unravelled by Maxine Hong Kingston in *The Woman Warrior*.

The impulse to excavate in no way diminishes in *China Men*. Or so Kingston's continuing prospectus suggests:

> I'd like to go to China if I can get a visa and—more difficult—permission from my family, who are afraid that applying for a visa would call attention to us: the relatives in China would get in trouble for having American capitalist connections, and we Americans would be put in relocation camps during the next witch hunt for Communists. Should I be able to convince my family about the good will of normalization, it's not the Great Wall I want to see but my ancestral village. I want to talk to Cantonese, who have always been revolutionaries, nonconformists, people who invented the Gold Mountain. I want to discern what it is that makes people go West and turn into Americans. I want to compare China, a country I made up, with what country is really out there.

But China or America, and whether 'made up' or actual, she again pursues both indefatigably. Her focus, this time, however, is 'China men' rather than 'China women', those of her own family, those she hypothesizes or invents, and those she cites from memory and acquaintance. What emerges, compellingly, is a genealogy, a Chinese-American equivalent of the founding Anglo-American mythus of Plymouth Rock, Jamestown, and the Pilgrim Fathers. Hers, however, delineates the transition not from Europe to America but from Han Mountain to Gold Mountain, the settling of America by the Chinese as acts both illegal (being smuggled aboard ships, using forged credentials, impersonating others) and legal (being processed respectively at Angel Island on the West Coast and Ellis Island in New York). The result, so to speak, becomes an unfolding scroll of cultural patrimony, America as possessed by the Chinese-American descendants of those 'three great mandarins' who sailed into the Bay of

Manila in 1603 to the amazement of the Filipinos, and, in turn, of even *their* mythical ocean-faring predecessors who rank alongside the Asian-Indians and Vikings as America's possible first discoverers.

The 'China Men' she invokes form a sequence: among them Great Grandfather Bak Goong, who worked the Hawaiian sugar plantations and returned to Han country with a new wife; Grandfather Ah Goong, who dug the land for the Central Pacific Railroad and took part in the bitter strike of 1867 ('He had built a railway out of sweat'); her own father Ba-Ba, born in San Francisco in 1903, laundryman and 'American father'; and her unnamed brother who fights in Vietnam only to return home a veteran unloved and unhonoured by his 'native' America. These lives she interweaves with others, not least those alluded to in a section called 'Laws' which chronicles the sorry history of anti-Chinese legislation (in fact general anti-Asian legislation) as embodied in bills like the Burlingame Treaty, the Scott Act, the Geary Act and the different Nationality, Exclusion and Segregation laws. It therefore reads as a special vindication of success against odds that a 'million or more' Chinese-Americans live in America spread from California to Alaska to New York and even into the South. The thread throughout the story is that of lineage and continuity, told both against an evolving background of pre-revolutionary, Maoist and post-Maoist China and of frontier and modern America. Like Anaya and Erdrich, Maxine Hong Kingston indeed tells an ethnic American story, yet also like them one so arrestingly re-imagined as to have made 'ethnic' the sign not of one story but that of all America.

NOTES

1. Broadcast 18 April 1989, and repeated 23 April 1989. The interviewer was the present writer.
2. Skow's review continues: 'The Chinese-American culture is only beginning to throw off . . . literary sparks, and Amy Tan's bright, sharp-flavored first novel belongs on a short shelf dominated by

Maxine Hong Kingston's remarkable works of a decade ago, *The Woman Warrior* and *China Men'—Time*, 27 March 1989.
3. See, respectively: Angie Debo, *A History of the Indians of the United States* (Norman: University of Oklahoma Press, 1970); Julian Samora and Patricia Vendel Simon, *A History of the Mexican-American People* (Notre Dame, Indiana: University of Notre Dame Press, 1977), and Lerone Bennet, Jr., *Before the Mayflower: A History of the Negro in America 1619–1964*, rev. edn. (Baltimore, Maryland: Penguin Books, 1966).
4. For a provocative contemporary cultural discussion of these issues see Werner Sollers, *Beyond Ethnicity: Consent and Descent in American Culture* (New York: Oxford University Press, 1986).
5. The following offer accounts of this achievement: James M. McPherson, Laurence B. Holland, James M. Banner, Nancy J. Weiss and Michael D. Bell (eds.), *Blacks in America: Bibliographical Essays* (New York: Doubleday, 1971); Roger Rosenblatt, *Black Fiction* (Cambridge, Massachusetts: Harvard University Press, 1974); Addison Gayle, Jr., *The Way of the New World: The Black Novel in America* (New York: Anchor/Doubleday, 1975); Michael S. Harper and R. E. Stepto (eds.), *Chants of Saints: A Gathering of Afro-American Literature, Art and Scholarship* (Urbana, Illinois: Illinois University Press, 1979); Robert Stepto, *From Behind the Veil: A Study of Afro-American Narrative* (Urbana, Illinois: Illinois University Press, 1979); A. Robert Lee (ed.) *Black Fiction: New Studies in the Afro-American Novel* (London: Vision Press, 1980); C. W. E. Bigsby, *The Second Black Renaissance: Essays in Black Literature* (Westport, Connecticut: Greenwood Press, 1980); A. Robert Lee, *Black American Literature Since Richard Wright* (British Association of American Studies Pamphlet No. 11, 1983); Keith E. Byerman, *Fingering the Jagged Grain: Tradition and Form in Recent Black Fiction* (Athens, Georgia: University of Georgia Press, 1985); and John F. Callaghan, *In the Afro-American Grain: The Pursuit of Voice in Twentieth-century Black Fiction* (Urbana, Illinois: University of Illinois Press, 1988).
6. On Chicano history and politics, see especially: Matt S. Meier and Feliciano Rivera, *The Chicanos: A History of Mexican Americans* (New York: Hill and Wang, 1972); Rodolfo Acuna, *Occupied America: The Chicano's Struggle Towards Liberation* (San Francisco: Canfield Press, 1972); Marcia T. García *et al* (eds.), *History, Culture and Society: Chicano Studies in the 1980s* (Ypsilanti, Michigan: Bilingual Press/ Editorial Bilingüe, National Association of Chicano Studies, 1983); John A. García *et al* (eds.), *The Chicano Struggle: Analyses of Past and Present Efforts* (Ypsilanti, Michigan: Bilingual Press/Editorial Bilingüe, National Association of Chicano Studies, 1984); Alfredo Mirandé, *The Chicano Experience: An Alternative Perspective* (Notre Dame, Indiana: University of Notre Dame Press, 1985); Rodolfo O. de la Garza, Frank D. Bean, Charles M. Bonjean, Ricardo Romo and Rodolfo Alvarez (eds.), *The Mexican American Experience*

(Austin, Texas: University of Texas Press, 1985); and Renate von Bardeleben, Dietrich Briesemeister and Juan Bruce-Novoa (eds.), *Missions in Conflict: Essays on U.S.: Mexican Relations and Chicano Culture* (Tubingen: Gunter Narr Verlag, 1986). For the Chicano literary renaissance, see: Ed Ludwig and James Santibañez (eds.), *The Chicanos: Mexican American Voices* (Baltimore, Maryland: Penguin Books, 1971); Francisco A. Lomelí and Donaldo W. Urioste, *Chicano Perspectives in Literature: A Critical and Annotated Bibliography* (Albuquerque, New Mexico: Pajarito Publications, 1976); Francisco Jiménez (ed.), *The Identification and Analysis of Chicano Literature* (Binghampton, New York: Bilingual Press/Editorial Bilingüe, National Association of Chicano Studies, 1979); Juan Bruce-Novoa, *Chicano Authors: Inquiry by Interview* (Austin, Texas: University of Texas Press, 1980); Juan Bruce-Novoa, *Chicano Poetry: A Response to Chaos* (Austin, Texas: University of Texas Press, 1982); Salvador Rodríguez del Pino, *La Novela Chicana Escrita en Español: Cinco Autores Comprometidos* (Ypsilanti, Michigan: Bilingual Press/Editorial Bilingüe, National Association of Chicano Studies, 1982); Jorge A. Huerta, *Chicano Theater: Theme and Forms* (Ypsilanti, Michigan: Bilingual Press/Editorial Bilingüe, National Association of Chicano Studies, 1982); Charles M. Tatum, *Chicano Literature* (Boston, Twayne Publishers, 1982); Robert G. Trujillo and Andrés Rodríguez, *Literatura Chicana: Creative and Critical Writings Through 1984* (Oakland, California: Floricanto Press, 1985); Luis Leal, *Aztlán y México: Perfiles Literarios e Históricos* (Binghampton, New York: Bilingual Press/Editorial Bilingüe, National Association of Chicano Studies, 1985); Cordelia Candelaria, *Chicano Poetry: A Critical Introduction* (Westport, Connecticut: Greenwood Press, 1986); Julio A. Martínez and Francisco A. Lomelí (eds.), *Chicano Literature: A Reference Guide* (Westport, Connecticut: Greenwood Press, 1986); and Carl R. Shirley and Paula W. Shirley, *Understanding Chicano Literature* (Columbia: University of South Carolina, 1988).

7. Leslie Fiedler, *The Return of the Vanishing American* (New York: Stein and Day, 1968); Dee Brown, *Bury my Heart at Wounded Knee: an Indian History of the American West* (New York, Holt, 1970).

8. For general accounts of this renaissance, see Jack W. Marken (ed.), *The American Indian Language and Literature* (Illinois: A.M.H. Publishing Corporation, Goldentree Bibliography, 1978); Robert F. Berkhover, Jr., *The White Man's Indian: Images of the American Indian from Columbus to the Present* (New York: Knopf, 1978); Charles R. Larson, *American Indian Fiction* (Albuquerque, New Mexico: University of New Mexico Press, 1978); Paula Gunn Allen (ed.), *Studies in American Indian Literature* (New York: Modern Language Association of America, 1983); Kenneth Lincoln, *Native American Renaissance* (Berkeley and Los Angeles: University of California Press, 1983); Brian Swann (ed.), *Smoothing the Ground: Essays on Native American Oral Literature* (Berkeley and Los Angeles: University of California Press, 1983); Arnold Krupat, *For Those*

Ethnic Renaissance

Who Come After: A Study of Native American Autobiography (Berkeley and Los Angeles: University of California Press, 1985); and Brian Swann and Arnold Krupat (eds.), *Recovering the Word: Essays on Native American Literature* (Berkeley and Lost Angeles: University of California Press, 1987).
9. For a relevant background, see H. Brett Melendy, *Chinese and Japanese Americans* (Boston: Twayne Publishers, 1972; reprinted New York: Hippocrene Books, 1984).
10. A most useful pamphlet which deals with these and other comic-strip ethnic stereotypes is: Charles Hardy and Gail F. Stern (eds.), *Ethnic Images in the Comics* (Philadelphia, Pennsylvania: Balch Institute for Ethnic Studies, 1986). See, also, Eugene Franklin Wong, *Visual Media Racism: Asians in the American Motion Pictures* (New York: Arno Press, 1978).
11. See, especially, Amy Tachiki, Eddie Wong, Franklin Odo, with Betty Wong (eds.), *Roots: An Asian American Reader* (Los Angeles: U.C.L.A. Asian American Studies Center, 1971); Kay-yu and Helen Palubinska (eds.), *Asian American Authors* (Boston: Houghton Mifflin, Co., 1972); Frank Chin, Jeffery Paul Chan, Lawson Fusso Inada and Shawn Hsu Wong (eds.), *Aiiieeee! An Anthology of Asian-American Authors* (Washington, D.C.: Howard University Press, 1974); Elaine H. Kim, *Asian American Literature: An Introduction to the Writings and their Social Context* (Philadelphia: Temple University Press, 1982); and King-Kok Cheung and Stan Yogi (eds.), *Asian American Literature, An Annotated Bibliography* (New York: Modern Language Association of America, 1988).
12. *Time*, 31 August 1988.
13. To these I would add: Raymond Barrio, *The Plum Pickers* (1969), Richard Vásquez, *Chicano* (1970), Miguel Méndez, *Peregrinos de Aztlán (Pilgrims of Aztlan*, 1971), Oscar Zeta Acosta, *The Auto-biography of a Brown Buffalo* (1972), Alexandro Morales, *Caras Viejas y Vino Nuevo (Old Faces and New Wine*, 1975), Rolando Hinojoso, *Klail City y sus Alredededos (Klail City and its Environs*, 1976), and Nash Candelaria, *Memories of the Alhambra* (1977).
14. The other two are *The Magic Journey* (1976) and *The Nirvana Blues* (1978).
15. *Bless Me, Ultima* (Berkeley, California: Quinto Sol Publications, 1972); *Heart of Aztlán* (Berkeley, California: Editorial Justa, 1976); and *Tortuga* (Berkeley, California: Editorial Justa, 1979). Among Anaya's other main publications should be included his several anthologies: *Cuentos: Tales from the Hispanic Southwest* (Santa Fe, New Mexico: Museum of New Mexico Press, 1980) and (co-ed. Antonio Marquez), *Cuentos Chicanos: A Short Story Anthology* (Albuquerque, New Mexico: University of New Mexico Press, 1984); his play *The Season of la Llorona* (produced by El Teatro de la Companía de Albuquerque, October 1979); his travel-narrative *A Chicano in China* (Albuquerque, New Mexico: University of New Mexico Press, 1986); his collection *The Silences of the Llano: Short*

163

Stories (1982); and his various essays and stories published in magazines like *Bilingual Review/Revista Bilingüe, Escolios, Agenda, Rocky Mountain Magazine, Grito del Sol* and *South Dakota Review.*
16. Juan Bruce-Novoa (ed.), *Chicano Authors: Inquiry by Interview* (op. cit.), pp. 184–85.
17. *Love Medicine* (New York: Holt, Rinehart & Winston, 1984), *The Beet Queen* (New York: Henry Holt & Co., 1986), and *Tracks* (New York: Henry Holt & Co., 1988). Equally Indian in its focus is the rightly acclaimed novel of Louise Erdrich's husband—Michael Dorris, *A Yellow Raft in Blue Water* (New York: Henry Holt and Company, 1987).
18. Cited as a dustjacket comment on *The Beet Queen.*
19. As full an account as any of this aspect of Indian experience can be found in Raymond William Stedman, *Shadows of the Indian: Stereotypes in American Culture* (Norman, Oklahoma: University of Oklahoma Press, 1982).
20. Maxine Hong Kingston, *The Woman Warrior: Memoirs of a Girlhood Among Ghosts* (New York: Vintage Books, 1977) and *China Men* (New York: Alfred A. Knopf, 1980).

7

Mean Streets, Mystery Plays: The New Pathology of Recent American Crime Fiction

by JULIAN G. HURSTFIELD

'History, history! We fools, what do we know or care? History begins for us with murder and enslavement, not with discovery.'
—William Carlos Williams, *In the American Grain* (1925)

'The fat man smiled complacently. "These are facts, historical facts, not school-book history, not Mr. Wells's history, but history nonetheless." '
—Dashiell Hammett, *The Maltese Falcon* (1930)

'Oh, gigantic paradox, too utterly monstrous for solution!'
—Edgar Allan Poe, 'William Wilson' (1839)

1

Crime, and murder in particular, did not only, as William Carlos Williams suggested, initiate American history; they also occupy a central place within American fiction and, it now seems, within the actual lives of American novelists.[1]

Significantly, many of the authors surveyed in Tony Tanner's *City of Words* (1971) have since had, as it were, their own brush with the law.[2] Truman Capote had already, in 1965, proposed a new direction for the novel by his meticulous reconstruction of one particular crime, in *In Cold Blood* (1965)[3]; he returned, in 1980, to what he subtitled 'A Nonfiction Account of an American Crime', in a novella, 'Handcarved Coffins', in which a series of murders in a small Western town remains, at the end, unavenged though not, by the narrator or the reader, unsolved: 'The way I look at it', the supposed murderer, never to be arraigned, says, 'it was the hand of God.'[4]

In the earlier novel, *In Cold Blood*, one aspect of Capote's literary power lay in his apparently personal witness to the commission of a crime, and also to the subsequent unfolding of American justice, the execution of two psychotic murderers; in this later novella, Capote's resolution is far more ambivalent: the author and the reader have discovered, as the fiction ends, what the mere processes of American law never will. The line between innocence and guilt (the narrator has made himself an accomplice) has come to be as vague as that between fact and fiction.

Norman Mailer has been no less interested in the details and mechanics of crime, and also in the psychopathology of criminality, its relationship to the larger activities of American society. After several journalistic explorations of violence,[5] he explored, in encyclopaedic detail, the life and mentality of Gary Gilmore, the first American convicted murderer to *request* the death penalty[6]; thence Mailer moved on to promote the literary work of a convicted murderer who, once paroled, murdered again[7]; and thence, Mailer wrote his most recent novel, *Tough Guys Don't Dance* (1984) as a spectacularly violent murder mystery.[8]

As American writers, Capote and Mailer are scarcely unique in their obsession with violence and murder. William Styron, for example, found himself, in 1961, preparing to protect a 24-year-old felon, Benjamin Reid, against the state of Connecticut's determination to execute him for murder; and Styron succeeded (only to have Reid escape from parole and commit a rape).[9] And towards the end of his own life James Baldwin found in the Atlanta Child Murders of 1980–82, and the subsequent trial and conviction of a black murderer of black children, an opportunity to renew his lifelong exploration of America's complex attitude towards racial justice.[10]

What is first notable about these writers' interest in crime is that it is in a particular sort of crime: violent, homicidal. Tom Wolfe first drew attention to this in an essay entitled 'Pornoviolence', where he wrote of Capote's *In Cold Blood*, that '. . . the book's suspense is based largely on a totally new idea in detective stories: the promise of gory details, and the withholding of them until the end.'[11] These writers are not, that is, much concerned with white-collar embezzlement or computer fraud. They rather display the novelist's traditional occupation with the relationship between the élite and the underworld, an interest as old as the novel itself, as exemplified by Fielding and Dickens.

But in American writing a recent shift does appear to have taken place. In a famous essay, first published in 1946, Lionel Trilling argued that Americans had a particular way of viewing reality: it was 'always material reality, hard, resistant, unformed, impenetrable, and unpleasant.'[12] Trilling was here attacking not so much Theodore Dreiser himself, but Dreiser's easy acceptance by a generation of literary critics as a truthful portrayer of social reality, and thus a literary artist. And Dreiser had acquired this respectful audience through his documentation of economic and sexual exploitation. But while he burrowed deep underground, uncovering numerous corruptions, he did not directly accost the issue of criminality.

Trilling's essay appears mild beside Philip Roth's 1960 essay (reprinted in 1975) 'Writing American Fiction'. Roth here describes the plight of the American novelist in attempting to portray American reality, and argues, in a sense *against* Trilling, that brutality and criminality have come to beggar the creative writer's imagination. He opens his essay with the example of a particularly foul crime, which really did occur, and then considers the ways in which some other contemporary writers have dealt with this problem. But what is notable is that it was precisely a crime, the murder of two teenage girls, which inspired his reflections on American reality.[13]

That particular murder occurred in Chicago; and it is

appropriate that Chicago's laureate, Saul Bellow, should choose, in the latest of his novels set in that city, *The Dean's December* (1982), to treat the level of criminal behaviour there as an index of the entire nation's health: and not only the level of crime, but its nature, its indiscriminate, sadistic, inhuman qualities. This is an example of a kidnapping:

> Towards daybreak of the second day, for reasons not explained in the record, Spofford Mitchell let Mrs. Sathers go, warning her not to call the police. He watched from his car as she went down the street. . . . She rang several doorbells, but no one would let her in. An incomprehensibly frantic woman at five in the morning—people wanted no part of her. They were afraid. As she turned away from the third or fourth closed door, Mitchell pulled up and reclaimed her. He drove to an empty lot, where he shot her in the head. He covered her body with trash.[14]

American writers have, it seems, been pursuing a concern with crime which is not marginal. Criminal behaviour seems to have moved to the centre of their interests. Nor is it hard to appreciate why. The events of the 1960s, and more especially the documentation about them which materialized in the 1970s, did indeed suggest that crime possessed a new prominence in American public life. A President is assassinated; so is his brother, a leading Presidential candidate, and so is the most prominent black politician in the world; in all cases the motives, and in one case even the identity, of the culprits remain obscure. A war is waged, and its very legality is questioned. A President is nearly impeached. All these events brought in their train a secondary cast of criminal, semi-criminal, even innocent defendants: President Kennedy's assassin's assassin or assassins, spies, informants, conspirators, draft-dodgers, war-protestors, burglars, phone-tappers.

These events also yielded up a series of *texts*—the 'Warren Commission Report on the Assassination of President John F. Kennedy' (1964), the 'Pentagon Papers' (1971), and the 'White House Tapes' (1974)—which certainly invite some literary, symptomatic criticism[15]; and at least one of these has received proper literary consideration. Don DeLillo's

Libra (1988) is the first novelistic treatment of the Kennedy assassination to be based upon the investigations of the specially convened House Select Committee on Assassinations (1979), though its slightly more recent source appears to be Anthony Summers's *Conspiracy* (1980).[16] In making the Kennedy assassination itself a subject for fiction, DeLillo proposes the literary imagination as the only realm within which America's most public mystery may be solved or resolved, in which any consolation for the public grief may be achieved. He does admit to the reader, in an Author's Note, that

> In a case in which rumours, facts, suspicions, official sub-terfuge, conflicting sets of evidence and a dozen labyrinthine theories all mingle, sometimes indistinguishably, it may seem to some that a work of fiction is one more gloom in a chronicle of unknowing.

But, he adds, 'because this book makes no claim to literal truth . . . readers may find refuge here'. Fiction works as a form of solace.

In fact the entire novel is built around the efforts of Nicholas Branch (the author's surrogate) actually to write a *book*, an account based on all the available documentation on the assassination, and to uncover a conspiracy that outreached itself to the point of self-destruction: supposed only to wound the President and thus, by implicating Castro's Cuba, strengthen America's anti-Castro resolve, the successful assassination merely enfeebles and unravels the anti-Castro movement. The lone assassin remains, accidentally, a lone assassin, emancipated from the conspiracy which sought to embrace him. But in the course of Nicholas Branch's inquiry much is learned about the relationship between fiction and murder:

> Plots carry their own logic. There is a tendency of plots to move toward death. He believed that the idea of death is woven into the nature of every plot. A narrative plot no less than a conspiracy of armed men. The tighter the plot of a story, the more likely it will come to death. A plot in fiction, he believed, is the way we localise the force of death outside the book, play it off, contain it. The ancients staged mock battles

to parallel the tempests in nature and reduce their fear of gods who warred across the sky. He worried about the deathward logic of his plot.[17]

If crime attracts, as never before, the attention of America's writers, and if criminal behaviour appears to be a permanent facet of American public life, then a case emerges for considering the work of writers for whom crime has not been merely a hobby, a distraction, a social concern, or a metaphor or synecdoche for wider preoccupations. Crime is a profession, and so is writing about crime. It is the argument of this essay that the last two decades have witnessed a shift in the way in which American crime writers have constructed their fictions, and that this shift has been occasioned by the events of these last years. It is a shift measurable in moral sensibility, in legal and political cynicism, and also in the new demands made upon fiction itself. If, that is, crime is so vital in American life, it may be worth consulting the experts.

2

'Organised crime' is one famous American contribution to the lexicon of criminal analysis. With the publication, in 1969, of Mario Puzo's *The Godfather*, this phenomenon, the Mafia, appeared to have found its Gibbon. Even before the 1972 film was released, the book had sold over 500,000 hard-cover and 10,000,000 paperback copies. A novel, it was often read as a *roman à clef*, which may account for a part of its astonishing popularity. But another part may also lie in its originality, its departure not only from the gangster films of the 1930s, but also from the traditional American way of viewing organized crime.[18]

This had been established as early as 1931 by Walter Lippmann in his articles on 'The Underworld as Servant', where he became the first writer to draw the distinction between the mere criminal (the burglar, say, who operates on a simple economic calculus) and organized crime, the underworld, which flourishes on its social function, pandering to prohibited appetites. *That* form of crime would always exist, Lippmann suggested, because Americans are too moral to tolerate human weakness, and because they are too great lovers of liberty to tolerate the tyranny which might make it possible to abolish what they prohibit. They have made laws which act like a protective tariff—to encourage the business of the underworld.[19]

But fantasies also were being encouraged by Puzo's novel, and Daniel Bell had railed against these as long ago as 1953, when he challenged 'the myth of the Mafia'. To Bell, the American public was being deceived if it was led to suppose that a tentacular organization controlled the violation of America's laws. The most that was occurring was a conventional ascent, along admittedly shady escalators, of a few members of a newly arrived, otherwise excluded immigrant group. Their ruthlessness and their economic warfare only echoed an earlier generation of Robber Barons; they differed only in confronting certain Anglo-Saxon taboos.[20]

The Godfather, novel or film (1972), is not, then, a work of realism. Its effects are felt at several other levels. It is, first, a family drama, in which filial loyalties pre-empt legal or moral obligations; in fact those loyalties *become* these obligations. Secondly, it is a chronicle of ethnic advancement within a prejudiced community. Then, too, it is a document about the submissive part played by women within a masculine, entrepreneurial world. The novel concludes with Kay, devout and obedient, saying 'the necessary prayers for the soul of Michael Corleone', her husband, whom she now recognizes as capable of mass murder[21]; but the second film, *The Godfather, Part II* (1974), with an original screenplay by Puzo and Francis Ford Coppola, has a newly resentful and rebellious Kay. The novel is also, as most viewers of the first film instantly recognize, a parable about the corporate world, an amoral, bloodthirsty Hobbesian state of nature. And, finally, it returns the reader to the Epic form, recapitulating, in Michael Corleone's trajectory, the pattern of the *Odyssey*—the succession from father to son, the necessary journeying, the belligerence, the avenge. It is for these reasons that one critic has referred to *The Godfather* as 'the world's most typical novel'.[22]

It may well be that, but what it is not is a realistic portrait of American crime.[23] It is, more accurately, a faithful rendering of the way Americans *view* crime, as if Puzo had absorbed, at last, the full meaning of Robert Warshow's 1948 reflections on 'The Gangster as Tragic Hero', which argued that the American perception of crime would never be at the level of social realism:

> What matters is that the experience of the gangster *as an experience of art* is universal to Americans. There is almost nothing we understand better or react to more readily or with quicker intelligence. . . . In ways that we do not easily or willingly define, the gangster speaks for us, expressing that part of the American psyche which rejects the qualities and the demands of modern life, which rejects 'Americanism' itself.[24]

Corporate crime, in Puzo's imaginative fiction, resembles corporate business; so too has law enforcement come to mirror law-breaking. The Federal Bureau of Investigation appears now to have lost its reputation for unimpeachable integrity; and one recent cultural historian has been able to date very precisely that moment when the F.B.I. lost its allure, 22 December 1975, when *Time* ran a cover story, 'The Truth About Hoover', documenting the quasi-legal activities in which the Bureau's director had been engaged.[25]

Puzo's novel was written several years before the connections between organized crime and Kennedy's assassination had been advanced. But American writers were already alive at least to the suspicion that criminal forces were at work in political life, and that these profited from moral and religious taboos. Consider the following passage:

> It would take an ideologist of the wildest sort to come up with an anti-capitalist satire which would reflect, quite accurately, the present situation of narcotics and the law. Take a substance which is, in nature, cheap, abundant, and addictive. Its addictive properties make it a seller's dream; its only drawback is its easy availability. There is no profit in it. Pass against the selling, production, cultivation, consumption, or possession of that substance the most stringent laws. Instantly, by virtue of being illegal, the substance

172

becomes rare and expensive. The law itself has created a situation in which there is an enormous, in fact incalculable, profit to be made for getting people, children for example, who would otherwise have no reason to consider narcotics, hooked.

This comes from a review published by Renata Adler in December 1977 of a book about the links between drugs, crime and political corruption.[26] But Adler reproduced that passage, almost word for word, in her 1983 novel *Pitch Dark*, her account of a woman's haunted drive across Ireland.[27] She only adds the following to her narrator's nervous reflections: 'The law generates a criminal apparatus which in turn generates a law-enforcement apparatus. With time, their personnel become the same.'[28] The same words hold true in fact and fiction. For if criminality were to thrive, now as in Victorian times, upon drugs, and if politicians themselves, then as now, thrived on the drug traffic, then public life, and in particular the arts, might well take on a hallucinogenic quality. 'Hashish' and 'assassin' have the same etymology.

3

At the other end of the scale to organized, corporate crime, the illegitimate offspring of Progressive mergers and New Deal conglomeration, lies an outpost of American individualism, the private detective, or 'eye' (or 'I' for investigator, observer, or author). This creation arose not in fact, but in the writings of Dashiell Hammett and Raymond Chandler as at once rational and moral. He solved mysteries and he upheld distinct values, usually those which challenged the surrounding corruption. Here too, just as Puzo revised American's understanding of organized crime, a shift has occurred: in the works of Robert Parker, Robert Crumley, Jonathan Valin and Roger Simon, amongst others, a different private eye has emerged, chastened by the defeats, the unsolved mysteries, and the moral complexities of the 1960s.

One way of measuring this change is to reconsider in full Chandler's famous remark about 'mean streets'. His words are '. . . down these mean streets a man must go, *who is not himself mean, who is neither tarnished nor afraid'*.[29] As in Martin Scorsese's 1973 film, *Mean Streets*, this prescription is often taken as a plea for social realism—of the kind that Trilling had deplored—a demand for brutal, sordid reality, graphically and explicitly conveyed. But Chandler always had, and may still possess, a genteel readership, and 'mean', as applied to a person as well as an environment, has several possible meanings. It does not only imply poverty and dereliction. It is also a unit of measurement, a standard ('moyen'), and that is certainly how Chandler meant it to apply to his hero, Philip Marlowe, who would rise above current standards.

Two original screenplays from the 1970s illustrate the distance which has been travelled from that particular rôle model. In Robert Towne's *Chinatown* (1974), his private detective, J. J. Gittes, has few moral qualities: he works, as Marlowe would never have done, on divorce cases, and he works as a mercenary. While he is intellectually capable of resolving a straightforward mystery (he is skilled at following a suspect, or at piecing clues together), and while he can uncover a villainy, even discover the identity of a murderer, he is disastrously inept at discerning the real evil—the child abuse, the incest—which is the pivot of the plot.

The film is set in the 1930s, and a 1930s audience would have expected a film entitled *Chinatown* to be set in Chinatown, even perhaps to be about Chinatown. But in the 1970s sensibility, Chinatown becomes a zone of consciousness, an ambience, the memory of a nightmare. It is where the host community of Los Angeles imports, and then only in the closing minutes, its moral corruption, its darkest Oedipal secrets; and a private detective, limited by his dependence on reason and logic, cannot even secure a small triumph.

In *Night Moves* (1974), Alan Sharp's original screenplay is even harsher on the private detective, Harry Moseby. For here it is precisely the detective's obsession with 'finding out', with applying reason to human affairs, which unravels his own life. We learn that he had searched for years for his father, only, having found him, never to speak to him. A rational discovery had been made, and that was sufficient. The 'need to know' which energized an earlier generation

174

of detectives has now become a moral weakness. It does not enable this detective to discover his wife's unfaithfulness, nor his new lover's murderousness, because these failings lie in a different realm, impervious to rational assault. Relying so much upon his investigative skills, he is powerless before moral and psychological confusions which defy reasoned enquiry. At the end, after several deaths—all of which could be attributed to his relentless prying—he is left wounded and alone in a stranded motor boat, which is literally moving in ever widening circles.

The writers who, in recent years, have re-animated private-eye fiction are well aware of an uneasy moral climate. Their creations suffer from Korean or Vietnamese battle fatigue; or they are disillusioned graduates of the 1960s counter-culture. This is to offer a new form of cynicism from a hard-boiled hero. Roger Simon's private detective, in *The Big Fix* (1973), suspends his investigations for a brief interlude with a prostitute: 'It had been a long time. Besides, who cared about a murder or a big election fix? They could wait.'[30] Jonathan Valin's Harry Stoner also possesses a remarkably pragmatic sense of morality:

> Sometimes it's useful to pretend that the world ought to be a better place than it is, even if it is an imperative founded exclusively on schoolboy good wishes and the quirks of the subjunctive mood.[31]

'In my business', James Crumley's protagonist confesses, 'you need a moral certitude that I no longer claim to possess.'[32]

One of the most revealing, because the most articulate, of these recent creations is Robert Parker's Spenser. His name of course is meant to suggest an affinity with Marlowe, but the differences, of generation and sensibility, are more striking. Spenser is undisputably tough, a weight-lifter and trained boxer; but he is also an intellectual who frequently quotes poetry; he is a gourmet chef; his girl friend is a social worker. As important, his moral code is hesitant and provisional. On one case he concludes that a runaway teenage girl, who has turned to prostitution, would actually be more secure working as a prostitute than returning to her

175

indifferent family, and he arranges a placement for her in a comparatively respectable and safe New York brothel:

> 'Maybe being a whore in fact is better than being a whore to the expectations of your neighbourhood', I said. . . . 'There's kinds of prostitution. Metaphorically the kinds are almost limitless. Everyone who does things for money instead of pride, I suppose.'
> Susan smiled at me. 'Didn't I see you building a cabin out by a pond in Concord the other day?'[33]

Paul Auster is not primarily a writer of crime fiction. But in *The New York Trilogy* (1985, 1986) he employed the private-eye genre to offer up a number of reflections upon changing literary and moral attitudes.[34] His particular concern is that staple of detective fiction, the missing person. But his narrators and his detectives do not discover very much, except how little they know about themselves. One of them writes detective fiction under the pseudonym William Wilson, which was of course the title of Edgar Allan Poe's 1839 allegory about the duality of human identity, the twinning of good and evil, conscience and selfhood.[35] Mainly his characters reminisce about literature and life; they make frequent allusions to the literary history and geography of New York; and they tell each other stories, anecdotes, fables. One of these stories concerns the search by a detective called Blue for a man called Gray:

> Gray had been missing for over a year, and his wife was ready to give him up for dead. Blue searched through all the normal channels and came up empty. Then, one day, as he was about to file his final report, he stumbled on Gray in a bar, not two blocks from where the wife was sitting, convinced he would never return. Gray's name was now Green, but Blue knew it was Gray in spite of this, for he had been carrying around a photograph of the man for the past three months and knew his face by heart. It turned out to be amnesia.[36]

This is, as Auster is well aware, a very old story. Its source is Hawthorne's 'Wakefield' (1835), those reflections triggered in the author's mind by a press report of a man who had left his wife for a period of twenty years, only to return as simply as he had departed, with no effort at explanation on either occasion. Wakefield also had chosen (initially,

Hawthorne conjectures, on a whim) simply to take some time to himself, but to remain in the same neighbourhood, observing life in his absence from it. And what Hawthorne drew from this bizarre event was the lesson that,

> Amid the seeming confusion of our mysterious world, indi-
> viduals are so nicely adjusted to a system, and systems to
> one another, and to a whole, that, by stepping aside for a
> moment, a man exposes himself to a fearful risk of losing his
> place forever.[37]

This story had not, before Auster, received its due as an influence upon mystery writing. Yet at a critical moment in *The Maltese Falcon*, just when Sam Spade is becoming involved with Brigid O'Shaughnessy, he tells her a similar, inexplicable story, about Flitcraft, a real-estate dealer who, one day, disappeared, ' "like that", Spade said, "like a fist when you open your hand" '. It turned out that a near accident, a falling beam, had pointed out to him the precariousness of his existence, and suggested the desirability of a change, a move away, if possible, from the random and the contingent: 'What disturbed him was the discovery that in sensibly ordering his affairs he had got out of step, and not into step, with life.'[38]

A generation later, and American detective writers begin to discern the limits of reason and logic and deduction. As Auster writes of one of his detectives, 'He has learned a thousand facts, but the only thing they have taught him is that he knows nothing.'[39] In a similar way, William Hjortsberg chose as his epigraph for *Falling Angel* (1979) the lines from Sophocles' *Oedipus the King*, 'Alas, how terrible is wisdom when it brings no profit to the man that's wise.' For this novel (filmed in 1987 as *Angel Heart*) has the format of a conventional private-eye fiction, but is actually a re-enactment of the Faustus legend. The solution to the mystery is that the detective's client is Lucifer.

4

I have been suggesting that the current mood in crime fiction, what may be seen as a new pathology, has been moving sharply away from realism. Mysteries remain unsolved, returned to that mystical, spiritual area which is the very root of the word 'mystery'; crimes go unpunished; reason does not prevail. If there is a source for this new tendency, it does not lie in the realism of the traditional novel, but in a particular feature of the Romantic movement. Hence those references to Hawthorne and Poe, to pre-modern conspiracies, already evident in Thomas Pynchon's *The Crying of Lot 49* (1966), to dark and irrational forces, some of them located in the human personality.[40]

Since 1933, with the publication of Mario Praz's *The Romantic Agony*, Romanticism has come to be viewed in a new way. It was now less a charming and affectionate idealization of the pre-modern world as a time of chivalry and chastity and honour. Its morbid side received a new emphasis, in which evil was at least the equal of good, in which sadistic appetites and erotic perversions inspired artistic achievement.[41] It has been the argument of this essay that the recent generation of crime writers have become, in some part, the heirs to this tradition. Confronted with so many unsolved (insoluble) mysteries, they have leap-frogged over the cosier realistic tradition, with its tidy confidence in reason and morality, and returned to an older, less comforting view of man's nature. To conclude, I shall consider one true, unsolved crime, and two fictional treatments of it.

On 15 January 1947 the body of Elizabeth Short was discovered in the weeds of a vacant lot in residential Los Angeles. She had been stabbed, tortured, and burned over a period of two or three days. Her throat had been cut from ear to ear; and her body had been cut in half. Her killer was never found, but the sensational nature of the crime, which came to be known as the Black Dahlia case (after the Raymond Chandler screenplay, *The Blue Dahlia*, 1946), has locked it into the Los Angeles, perhaps the American, folk-memory.[42] It is a modern counterpart to Poe's 'The Mystery of Marie Roget'.[43]

John Gregory Dunne's 1977 novel, *True Confessions*, employs this crime to open up a significantly modern world of corruption. He does note in a Foreword, 'The author is aware of the anachronisms and ambiguities in the social and cultural punctuation of this book, as he is aware of distortions of time and geography.' That may be a modernist approach towards narrative, but Dunne also uses a very old motif: the two brothers who grow up into different and opposed professions. In the 1930s, in films such as *Angels with Dirty Faces* (1938), the choice was between gangster and priest. In the 1970s the choice is between policeman and priest, and it is the priest who becomes the more corrupt, deeply implicated in the financial misdoings of the Roman Catholic hierarchy, one of whose patrons might be the Black Dahlia's murderer. In fact, since this is an unsolved murder, the crime goes unpunished; the killer appears to have been himself killed in a car crash a few moments after leaving the scene. But the detective only realizes this coincidence under the influence of his wife's crazed conversation, which wanders from topic to topic without any logical connection: 'Lineal thinking was irrelevant when you tried to follow Mary Margaret. You followed the bouncing ball.'[44] That was how mysteries were solved.

James Ellroy's approach to the crime, in *The Black Dahlia* (1987), is significantly different, though he too must let the culprit go unpunished, and he too has his detective solve the mystery through intuition, not logic. The vital discovery here is of a painting inspired by Victor Hugo's 1869 novel, *The Man Who Laughs*. That novel is certainly one of the most bizarre works of French literature ever published. But its central image—of a hideously mutilated man whose face is locked in a permanent grin—serves Ellroy's purpose well. He was enabled to write, in the 1980s, about a murder of the 1940s, which may have been inspired, in its goriest details, by a novel of the 1860s.[45]

Ellroy and Dunne are not alone among modern writers in finding in the past—even in the unsolved mysteries of the past—some comfort in an uncertain present. That is one of the positive legacies of Romanticism, offsetting somewhat its more disturbing Gothic qualities: its fascination with the darker aspects of human nature, its loss of faith in human reason. This awareness, even embrace, of moral confusion and intellectual inadequacy constitutes a new direction in crime fiction. It is also at a very large remove from the popular Romanticism of the Kennedy era. This is Camelot's underside, its aftermath.

NOTES

1. William Carlos Williams, *In the American Grain* (1925, reprinted Harmondsworth: Penguin, 1971), p. 55.
2. Tony Tanner, *City of Words* (London: Jonathan Cape, 1971).
3. Truman Capote, *In Cold Blood* (New York: Signet, 1965).
4. Truman Capote, 'Handcarved Coffins', in *Music for Chameleons* (London: Abacus, 1981), pp. 61–134; the quotation is on the last page.
5. For example, in *Advertisements for Myself* (London: Panther, 1959).
6. Norman Mailer, *The Executioner's Song* (London: Hutchinson, 1979).
7. Jack Henry Abbott, *In the Belly of the Beast* (New York: Knopf, 1981).
8. Norman Mailer, *Tough Guys Don't Dance* (London: Michael Joseph, 1984).
9. William Styron, *This Quiet Dust and Other Writings* (London: Jonathan Cape, 1983), pp. 137–70.
10. James Baldwin, *Evidence of Things Not Seen* (London: Michael Joseph, 1986).
11. Tom Wolfe, *Mauve Gloves and Madmen, Clutter and Vine* (New York: Farrar, Strauss and Giroux, 1976), pp. 157–65; the quotation is on pp. 163–64.
12. Lionel Trilling, *The Liberal Imagination* (Harmondsworth: Penguin, 1970), pp. 17–34; the quotation is on p. 26.
13. Philip Roth, *Reading Myself and Others* (London: Jonathan Cape, 1975), pp. 117–35: see also the references to this essay by Henry Claridge on p. 10, and Graham Clarke on p. 5.
14. Saul Bellow, *The Dean's December* (London: Michael Joseph, 1982), p. 194.
15. All Washington D.C.
16. DeLillo, *Libra* (New York, Viking, 1988); *Report of the House Select Committee on Assassinations* (Washington D.C., Government Printing Office, 1979); Anthony Summers, *Conspiracy, Who Killed President Kennedy?* (London: Fontana, 1980).
17. Don DeLillo, *Libra*, p. 221.
18. Mario Puzo, *The Godfather* (London: Heinemann, 1969).
19. Walter Lippmann, 'The Underworld as Servant', *Forum* (January, February, 1931), reprinted in Francis A. J. Ianni and Elizabeth Reuss-Ianni (eds.), *The Crime Society: Organised Crime and Corruption in America* (New York: Meridian, 1976), pp. 162–72; the quotation is on p. 171.
20. Daniel Bell, 'Crime as an American Way of Life', *The Antioch*

The New Pathology of Recent American Crime Fiction

Review (June 1953), reprinted in Ianni and Reuss-Ianni, Crime Society, pp. 99–107.
21. Puzo, Godfather, p. 448.
22. Marianna De Marco Torgovnick, 'The Godfather as the World's Most Typical Novel', South Atlantic Quarterly (Spring 1988) 87:2.
23. For the most recent corrective, see Michael Woodiwiss, Crime, Crusades and Corruption: Prohibitions in the United States, 1900–1967 (London: Pinter, 1988).
24. Robert Warshow, 'The Gangster as Tragic Hero', The Immediate Experience: Movies, Comics, Theatre, and Other Aspects of Popular Culture (New York: Atheneum, 1979), pp. 127–33; the quotation is on p. 30 (italics in original).
25. Richard Gid Powers, G-Men: Hoover's FBI in American Popular Culture (Carbondale: Southern Illinois University Press, 1983), pp. 282–84.
26. Renata Adler, 'Reflections on Political Scandal', a review of Edward Jay Epstein, Agency of Fear: Opiates and Political Power in America (New York: Putnam, 1977) in New York Review (8 December 1977).
27. Renata Adler, Pitch Dark (New York: Knopf, 1983), p. 115.
28. Raymond Chandler, 'The Simple Art of Murder', in Pearls are a Nuisance (Harmondsworth: Penguin, 1964), p. 198, italics added.
29. Roger Simon, The Big Fix (New York: Warner, 1973), p. 149.
30. Jonathan Valin, Final Notice (London: Collins, 1981), p. 16.
31. James Crumley, The Last Good Kiss (New York: Pocket Books, 1978), p. 8.
32. Robert B. Parker, Ceremony (Harmondsworth: Penguin, 1983), pp. 148–49.
33. Paul Auster, The New York Trilogy (single volume edition, London: Faber, 1987).
34. The Complete Tales and Poems of Edgar Allan Poe (Harmondsworth: Penguin, 1982), pp. 626–41.
35. Auster, New York Trilogy, pp. 139–40.
36. Nathaniel Hawthorne, Tales and Sketches (Library of America edition, 1982) pp. 290–98.
37. Dashiel Hammett, The Four Great Novels (London: Picador, 1982), pp. 428–30.
38. Auster, New York Trilogy, p. 170.
39. William Hjortsberg, Falling Angel (London: Hutchinson, 1979).
40. Thomas Pynchon, The Crying of Lot 49 (London: Jonathan Cape, 1967).
41. Mario Praz, The Romantic Agony (Oxford University Press, 1933).
42. Martin J. Wolf and Katherine Mader, L.A. Crime (London: Equation, 1989), pp. 175–77.
43. Complete Tales and Poems, pp. 169–207.
44. John Gregory Dunne, True Confessions (New York: Pocket Books, 1977), pp. 175–77.
45. James Ellroy, The Black Dahlia (New York: Mysterious Press, 1987).

Notes on Contributors

HENRY CLARIDGE is a lecturer in English and American literature at the University of Kent, where he also teaches in the American Studies programme. He has taught at the Universities of Indiana and Massachusetts and has written on American autobiography, Chicago, and Upton Sinclair. He contributes, with the editor of this volume, to the *Year's Work in English Studies*.

GRAHAM CLARKE is a lecturer in English and American literature at the University of Kent, where he also teaches in the American Studies programme. He has taught at the University of Colorado and has held fellowships at Brown and Yale. He has written on a range of subjects, amongst the most recent, articles on T. S. Eliot, Alfred Stieglitz, and American landscape painting. He is the editor of *The American City: Literary and Cultural Perspectives* (in the Critical Studies series) and of a four-volume critical anthology entitled *T. S. Eliot: Critical Assessments*. His book *Walt Whitman: The Poem as Private History* will be published by Vision Press/St. Martin's Press in 1990.

PETER DOUGHTY is Head of Modern Studies at Crewe + Alsager College of Higher Education, where he also teaches courses in English and American Studies. He has been an exchange professor in Pennsylvania, and, representing the Cambridge Examinations Syndicate, has visited a number of State Colleges in Nigeria to moderate Basic Studies programmes.

JULIAN G. HURSTFIELD is a lecturer in History at the University of Kent, and the author of *America and the French Nation, 1939–1945*. In 1985–86 he was a Fulbright Scholar, and an American Studies Fellow of the American Council of Learned Societies. He has also taught at Indiana University and at the University of Maryland. His essay, 'The Truths of Washington, D.C.' was included in *The American City*.

A. ROBERT LEE is Senior Lecturer in English and American Literature at the University of Kent at Canterbury. He is editor of the Everyman *Moby-Dick* (1975) and of eleven collections in the Critical Studies series, among the most recent: *Herman Melville: Reassessments* (1984); *Edgar Allan Poe: The Design of Order* (1986); *First Person Singular: Studies in American Autobiography* (1988); *Scott Fitzgerald: The Promises of Life* (1989); and *William Faulkner: The Yoknapatawpha Fiction* (1990). His *James Baldwin: Climbing to the Light* will appear in 1990.

ERIC MOTTRAM is Professor of English and American Literature at King's College, University of London. He is the author of many works on twentieth-century American writers and of numerous essays on aspects of American literature and culture, including *William Burroughs: The Algebra of Need*, *William Faulkner: A Profile*, and *The Rexroth Reader*. His most recent publications include a collection of essays, *Blood on the Nash Ambassador* and his *Collected Poems*.

DAVID SEABROOK is a graduate of the University of Kent and has written on Raymond Carver. He has a particular interest in recent American literature. He lives and works in Kent.

Index

Index

185

ACI 0672

3/5/92

PS
225
N48
1990